Social Policy and Social Services

Social Policy and

Consulting Editors: S. M. Miller New York University
Martin Rein Massachusetts Institute of Technology

Random House Series in Social Policy

Social Services

Alfred J. Kahn Columbia University School of Social Work

Random House New York

Library of Congress Cataloging in Publication Data

Kahn, Alfred J   1919–
Social policy and social services.

(The Random House series in social policy)
Bibliography: p.
1. Social service—United States.   2. United
States—Social policy.   I. Title.
HV91.K3   361'.973   72-12767
ISBN 0–394–31388–7

Typography by Karin Gurski Batten

Manufactured in the United States of America. Composed by Cherry Hill Composition, Pennsauken, N.J. Printed and bound by The Halliday Lithograph Corp., West Hanover, Mass.

First Edition

987

Preface

This book supplants chaos with order. The social services have been a jumbled, controversial area—attacked for the effectiveness of their methods and subsequently defended against such assaults; confused about their purposes; beset by difficult choices among contrasting principles; and disturbed over issues of appropriate organizational form. Alfred J. Kahn has charted a way through this swamp, not by a fixed line of advocacy of a staked-out position, but by codifying and clarifying conflicting positions, weighing the evidence where there is any, indicating needed research, and reconciling the reconcilable and isolating the irreconcilable. And, yet, he has managed to convey his vision of what the field should be like.

Why are the social services in such chaos? The 1960s, the period of the war on poverty, were both the health of the social services, since these personal services grew enormously and rapidly, and the disease of the social services, since the growth was fragmented and tumultuous—a metastasis rather than a plan. In the war on poverty the social services were assigned an enormous role, for they operated as the major strategy (or, more accurately, chance) for improving the situation of the poor. Too much was asked of the social services, for they could not compensate for the absence of programs to provide adequate cash support for individuals outside the labor market and of national economic actions to provide decent quality employment for those in the labor market. The swiftly emerging desire of minorities for autonomy and power made participation in the operation of social services a cardinal issue. The social services became enmeshed in the political-analytical research argument about the relative importance of individual defects and characteristics (often misleadingly presented as "the culture of poverty") or external constraints (unemployment, poor housing, inadequate welfare payments) as causes of poverty. Utilitarianism and rationalism were sweeping away the older concerns with decent standards of life for people, even if a better life did not improve their ability to get a job. They also combated pragmatism and empiricism in judging the effectiveness of programs whose consequences were inherently difficult to measure and in choosing among alternative ways of accomplishing goals. The methods of the economist were threatening the values of the social worker and humanitarian.

Political resistance to selective emphasis on blacks grew as the economy inflated and then was deflated and as welfare expenditure increases made effectiveness and cost prime issues in the social services. The very purposes of the services were attacked —for should they not be declining rather than expanding with rising income levels in the nation as a whole? The continuing existence of poverty amid affluence, as public money was being spent on the poor, made suspect those programs aimed at aiding the poor.

Kahn shows us where we are now with these issues and makes clear why they will not fade away. These issues pose fundamental questions about the purpose, character, and size of the social services in late capitalist societies. Underlying them is the inescapable, disturbing, difficult-to-put-at-rest conflict of principles: is the nation to be directed toward reducing inequalities and toward collective public consumption, or is greater equality a second-order goal, while the augmentation of private incomes is the first-order goal?

Debates about both issues are of growing and wide importance in contemporary America and other societies. They involve the level and impact of taxation, the composition of our gross national product, and the assigning of priorities among growth-inflation-

unemployment-distributive issues. Kahn has made the analysis of
the social services a microcosm of many of the basic questions now
facing American society. He has taken the social services from an
enclave position within the vast social welfare network and shown
how their future will be shaped by the American future. In doing
so, he reveals many of the choice points for all of American
society.

S. M. Miller

Martin Rein

Contents

Introduction

Prologue

The Need to Think About Social Services

This book is about social services—what they are and what questions must be answered in deciding what they will become. The goal is to inform citizens about issues and to guide students and scholars in pursuing them, not to advocate a comprehensive viewpoint.

The United States faces major issues of social service policy. For all its rhetoric and subsequent innovation, the American antipoverty war of the 1960s began as a social service strategy. The emphasis shifted from the social services usually employed to "rehabilitate" the poor—traditional family and child welfare, probation, and clinical services—to education, job counseling, and training; but the approach was nonetheless historically continuous with earlier "service" responses to social problems. By increasing skills and motivation and eliminating or decreasing difficulties in personal functioning, society would help people improve their situations.

In subsequent years[1] this orientation came under attack. On the one side were those who urged substitution of an "incomes strategy" instead. Their proposals, which had only limited impact, culminated in the appearance of the Report of the President's Commission on Income Maintenance Programs[2] and the Nixon Family Assistance Plan. More successful were those who preferred emphasis on political activation of the poor, especially poor blacks, on the assumption that only a shift in political power would eventually produce adequate resource redistribution to abolish poverty. Theirs was the path of "maximum feasible participation," for which income as well as service strategies were vehicles, not ends.

Social services continued, of course, as new approaches were enacted or proposed and some—day care, Head Start, family planning, specialized manpower efforts, services to the aged—expanded considerably. But for a while they were in eclipse among antipoverty warriors and reformers and were held in contempt by self-styled "revolutionaries." A policy judgment had been made.[3]

However, despite this recent history, advocates of improved and expanded social services are by no means all opponents of other social strategies. Late in 1968 a federal task force report on social services urged that services not be considered as a substitute for cash and called for large-scale consumer involvement in policy development, programming, and the rendering of services.[4] At the same time the report illustrated the complexity of the policy and programming issues that must be faced by those who would expand and improve social services even in a context that posits satisfactory income maintenance and consumer participation. Issues of universalism or selectivity, of service type and priority, of delivery system and staffing, of coordination and administration, all need to be faced. And the existence of significant need for social services on the American scene leaves little doubt that such expansion and improvement are, indeed, essential.[5]

I employ the term "social service" in these early paragraphs as though there were universal clarity as to what is meant. The fact is that social services are difficult to define because the concept carries ideological baggage and because social services are in transition. The problem of definition is discussed more fully in Chapter 1. For present purposes social services may be seen as communal provision to promote individual and group well-being and to aid those in difficulty. Thus, broadly defined, social services encompass health, education, and public housing, as well as such programs as family and child welfare, services to the aging, and the various counseling and assistance programs in schools, hospitals, and similar facilities. In present context, however, the larger, separately institutionalized systems, particularly health, income supports, housing and education, are excluded and the analysis focuses on the developmental, helping, and access services which remain. I call these latter "general social services"; the British refer to them as "personal social services."

The present monograph offers an introduction for those who would think about the organization, improvement, and expansion of social services. It begins by clarifying concepts and then turns to questions of scale, cost, and effectiveness. The major focus is on issues of social policy inherent in all major considerations about social services in the more constricted sense. While no effort is made to "sell" a perspective, my general orientation is apparent in the posing of issues and the guidance offered for their resolution. The final section, concentrating as it does on problems of social service organization and delivery, deals with current administrative, staffing, and practice questions and with specific efforts at innovation. It seeks to illustrate the relationship of policy to program and the complexity of achieving "payoff" even after a policy decision.

What, then, is the problem addressed? Why is there concern with social service policy and practice? While vocabularies and explanatory concepts vary, there is an astonishing range of agreement that social services are in need of major reform in the United States (and, for that matter, in Great Britain and many other countries as well) and that the reform, to be relevant, must not ignore certain basic issues.[6]

In this country, social services are often and justifiably characterized as inadequate in amount, range, and quality. A listing of service categories in any community may seem reasonably comprehensive, but a counting of quantity or an analysis of users is likely to reveal less than tokenism. For example: an inquiry about provision for homemakers discloses that there are "some" in almost every city. But twelve or fifty or even one hundred homemakers in a city of one million is meaningless, as is one small group residence for adolescents or three family service agencies employing twenty caseworkers. In another field—and it could have been any one of many—the Gerontological Society reported in 1968 as follows: ". . . to date, no community in the United States has developed a comprehensive network of services for the aging and the aged." Services, the society stated, are inadequate in volume and range and, where they exist, are often inaccessible.[7]

Similarly, there is little "depth" or diversity in the social service "repertoire," where circumstance calls for flexibility and options. Child welfare may mean foster homes or institutional care only, but not the generally conceded needed diversity of support to help families stay together. Probation may connote supervision of delinquents and monitoring of their activities, but not the required range of community interventions to assure their reintegration as full-fledged participants. For the aging there may be a senior citizens' center or a nursing home, but not the help for a productive post-retirement role, suited to individual circumstance.

Nor do available services necessarily reflect the high-quality models of the professional journals or the Sunday supplements. Users may confront drab waiting rooms, uninterested staffs, poorly trained personnel, insensitive treatment teams, ambiguous helping strategies. An agency's client may lose confidence in his family counselor; a child may refuse to confide in "his" foster-care worker. The community center group leader may be perceived as insensitive to the needs of the senior citizens with whom he works, and so on. I cannot report a quality "batting average" for each type of social service, but there is evidence that users and potential users, community observers, friends and relatives, and accrediting or licensing bodies often have good reason to be concerned about the quality of the personal help rendered to people in trouble.

Despite these limitations, many more people apparently would make use of social programs if they knew about them or, if knowing, they could gain entry.

Finally, there are the elusive matters of "imagery" and "stigma" that attach to social programs. Services, which employ the language of "helping," often seem to emphasize control of populations and problems rather than genuine assistance. They often seem to reflect moral attitudes and social evaluations that may be characterized as "blaming the victims." Simultaneously, through a process that may appear illogical but that apparently has social psychological validity, the persons who staff such services are also stigmatized and even attacked, as though they have engendered the problems or deviance they have been assigned to cure or to control. Even modern industrial societies would execute the messengers who convey bad tidings.

In short, only the most naïve of proponents believes that improvement of social services hinges solely on quantitative expansion. However, the raising of standards that apply to currently available services and the improvement of access will not be sufficient as response to the present state of the general social service system.

The manifest task also goes beyond assurance of equality for and equal responsiveness to all categories of potential users. The social scene is changing rapidly in ways especially relevant for social service planners. New concepts of rights and social priorities emerge, along with new recognition of and definitions of human need. Self-organized citizens increasingly raise questions about the responsiveness of services in type and form of organization to changing needs and differential needs among populations. Such questions arise as: What are current standards of urban amenity? What types of social services will best assist disadvantaged citizens to become fully participating community members? What are the service requirements and priorities of above-poverty citizens, of middle-class suburbanites; or should the community invest in services for such people at all?

He who would act with reference to service quantity, quality, relevance, or access also soon discovers that no single agency can proceed alone. Services are, or are said to be, interdependent, relating in many instances to others in an apparently logical interventive sequence (wherever they are located physically) and interacting with programs in their geographic proximity as well. Since social services are publicly supported, whether through direct or indirect financing, proposals for improvement often stress program and policy coordination.[8] More recently, students of social service organization have asked whether the creation of large and controlling coordinating structures, or what Roland Warren, in an industrial analogy, calls "cartelization," is necessarily the path of social service reform and have explored competition and other market-mechanisms as the route to improved social service provision and delivery. Still other analysts have argued that, while social services cannot succeed unless they are part of an organized network, a variety of approaches appear viable to achievement of a network that protects local options.

Consideration of the expansion and improvement of social services also leads to questions of resources, knowledge, and skill:
What can the society afford? How much do we know? What do we
know how to do? What are the requirements inherent in the doing?
And underlying any social strategy, questions of value, priority,
and social thrust are equally urgent, or even more important.
Strategy, direction, and posture ultimately emerge as *policy*—the
wedding of reality assessment and choice, of empiricism and
preference—and it is policy that is the focus of this monograph.
I conceive of policy as the explicit or implicit core of principles,
or the continuing line of decisions and constraints, behind specific
programs, legislation, administrative practices, or priorities. This
work concentrates on major policy options facing general social
services and on the connections between the choice of specific
options and the implementation (programming) strategies that
follow. The discussion begins with some foundations of definition
and fact.*

NOTES

1. For detail, see Alfred J. Kahn, *Studies in Social Policy and Planning.*
   (New York: Russell Sage Foundation, 1969), Chapter 2.
2. *Poverty Amid Plenty* (Washington, D.C.: Government Printing Office,
   1969).
3. Alfred J. Kahn, with the research assistance of Ruth A. Teitelbaum, "Do
   Social Services Have a Future in New York?," constituting the *City
   Almanac* (New York: New School for Social Research, February 1971).
4. *Services for People,* Report of the Task Force on Organization of Social
   Services (Washington, D.C.: Department of Health, Education, and Welfare, 1968).
5. Ibid. Yet, as we go to press, the debate continues to rage: service for
   the poor—or all Americans; "workfare" or developmental programs?

*Of necessity, policy questions of great importance to society, but not specific
to general social services or of great direct impact upon them, must be by-
passed. Nor is this a volume about method in policy development, for which the
reader is referred to the following, which, in turn, contain extensive bibliogra-
phies: Kahn, *Theory and Practice of Social Planning*; Raymond A. Bauer and
Kenneth J. Gergen (eds.), *The Study of Policy Formation* (New York: Free Press,
1968); Robert A. Dahl and Charles E. Lindblom, *Politics, Economics, and Welfare* (New York: Harper Torchbooks, 1963); Ira Sharkansky (ed.), *Policy Analysis
and Political Science* (Chicago: Markham Publishing Co., 1970); Yehezkel Dror,
Public Policy Making Reexamined (San Francisco: Chandler Publishing Co.,
1968), see esp. bibliographic essay, pp. 327–356.

For illustration, see the several papers in *Public Welfare*, 30, 1 (Winter 1972).

6. *Services for People*, Report of the Task Force on Organization of Social Services; also, Kahn, *Studies in Social Policy and Planning*, Chapter 6, and *Theory and Practice of Social Planning*, Chapter 10 (New York: Russell Sage Foundation, 1969); Elaine Cumming, *Systems of Social Regulation* (New York: Atherton, 1968); Robert Perlman and David Jones, *Neighborhood Service Centers* (Washington, D.C.: Government Printing Office, 1967); *Report of the Committee on Local Authority and Allied Personal Social Services* (Seebohm Report, Cmnd. 3703) (London: Her Majesty's Stationery Office, 1968); Gilbert Y. Steiner, *The State of Welfare* (Washington, D.C.: The Brookings Institution, 1971); William Ryan, *Blaming the Victim* (New York: Pantheon, 1971); and William A. Robson and Bernard Crick (eds.), *The Future of the Social Services* (Baltimore: Penguin, 1970).

7. *Encyclopedia of Social Work, Sixteenth Issue* (New York: National Association of Social Workers, 1971), Vol. 1, pp. 67–68.

8. The Seebohm Report offers a recent example. An earlier effort is illustrated by Alfred J. Kahn, *Planning Community Services for Children in Trouble* (New York: Columbia University Press, 1963).

1

The Terrain,
General Social Services

Such terms as social services, social welfare, and social work tend
to take on somewhat different meanings in different political and
cultural contexts. They are also variously employed depending
upon a country's stage of economic development. Given these differences, and in the interest of clarity, we must arrive at some
definitions that will serve this presentation.

What, then, are social services in the sense of the present
monograph? Let us begin with an illustrative case situation:

The Carlicks are a low-income working-class family. Mr. Carlick is a
semiskilled worker in a lumber yard. His wife, a housewife, devotes
her days to their four children, ranging from eighteen months to five
years of age. The oldest attends kindergarten. Not long ago, on a Sat-
urday morning, Mrs. Carlick was not well. After a few hours she sent
the five-year-old to knock at a neighbor's door. By the time Mr. Carlick

got home his wife was in bed, with the children in the next room, the neighbor having helped as much as possible, given her own large family. Mr. Carlick phoned the doctor. His wife needed an appendectomy. Arrangements were made for emergency hospitalization.

Mr. Carlick would care for the children on Sunday, a free day. He had no choice about Monday, even though he lost a day's pay and his employer told him that he had to be at work on Tuesday. What could he do? In this instance, recalling a sister's experience, he telephoned her and subsequently went to a voluntary sectarian family service agency. A homemaker was provided for child care and homemaking for the duration of the hospitalization. Mr. Carlick thus had access to a so-called "preventive" social service, the homemaker, where others must often place children in temporary shelters (another social service) under similar circumstances.

The experience actually opened yet another social service contact for this family. In a conversation with the hospital medical social worker, as she began to recover, Mrs. Carlick asked for some advice about the second oldest child, who seemed in many ways "slow." The social worker arranged for a clinic visit for assessment at a later point, after Mrs. Carlick returned home.

This is not a very gripping story, but it is more typical than the occasionally dramatic case that might be offered. For the particular family, of course, the services were of great importance.* Picture the difference between the experiences of four young children with the homemaker and the alternative of living in a large custodial shelter for two weeks, away from family and probably separated from one another, not understanding what it meant or whether family life would be resumed again. Consider the difference for the mother in the hospital—not fully relaxed, with a strange woman in charge, she had far more peace of mind to concentrate on her own medical treatment than if the family had to be broken up to permit the operation. In fact, it is unlikely that this father would have permitted the temporary placement of his young children. His job, therefore in jeopardy, was saved by the homemaker.

Nor should one underestimate the potential value of the diagnostic assessment of the mildly retarded child, an assessment initiated through the medical social work contracts.

In a relatively narrow sense, as often employed in the United

---

*Of no small significance, too, is the fact that the homemaker was far less expensive for the community than almost all the alternatives.

States and as used in the present volume, the term "social services" includes activities such as the following:

1. Day-care and similar child development and child-care programs (Head Start, family day care for infants, after-school
   care, and so on)
2. Homemakers and home helps
3. Personal and family guidance and counseling, including marital
   counseling
4. Child welfare activities such as foster care, adoption, protective services for neglected and abused children
5. Assessments for courts, schools, camps of parental relationships (are parents neglectful? with which member of a separated couple should a child reside?) or of a child's personality
   and capacities (is he capable of adjusting to a normal group?)
6. Big Brother, Big Sister, and related volunteer helping and guidance efforts
7. Probation and parole work
8. Family planning services
9. Community centers for the aged, for youth, for families
10. "Meals-on-wheels," "senior citizen" programs, special protec-
    tive programs for the aged
11. A diversity of group programs such as therapeutic group work
    with adolescents, organization of tenants in a housing project,
    organization of parents of retarded children.
12. Food stamps and school breakfast and lunch programs or sur-
    plus commodity distribution
13. Rural welfare programs and special programs for migrant
    laborers
14. Special programs to counsel potential migrants or immigrants
    and to help them adjust in new surroundings
15. Assistance to residents of poverty areas or members of under-
    privileged population groups, so that they may come together
    for mutual aid activity
16. Information, advice, referral, complaint, and advocacy services
    of many kinds.
17. Institutional programs for the neglected, dependent, disturbed
    (state training schools, homes for the aged, residential treat-
    ment for children, and so on)

Before examining more formal definitions of social services or
attempting to classify such services by types, some historical and

social perspectives may be helpful. It will not otherwise be clear why and in what sense the above listing may constitute a field and why there are both broader and narrower listings that are also employed. Nor will the derivation of some of the policy questions, subsequently introduced, be clear without such background.

Social Services in Industrial and Post-Industrial Societies

Social services appear everywhere in the modern world. They continue to exist and even expand as productivity increases and as average standards of living are raised. Indeed, they are seen as part of the improved standards. Thus, quite contrary to the assumptions of a laissez-faire social ethic, social services are hardly marginal or transitional programs. To comprehend this fully it is useful to discuss the *manifest,* the apparent, the conscious functions of social services as well as the *latent,* less visible, hidden functions.

If the point of departure is the agrarian life of the preindustrial society, the task of the social services in an urban and industrial world is to contribute to personal and group development and socialization as a substitute for what the community as a whole or the extended family once did. Families in the rural economy were tightly knit units for production, protection, distribution, consumption, socialization, and control, which turned to outside institutions only to settle matters among them and between them and their God, for defense against outsiders, and for the minimum of essential trade.

The specialization of modern life gives the family a much more circumscribed role, a subject to which many scholars have devoted considerable attention. The family as an economic unit has given way to specialized, usually large, organizations in which any given individual has a limited assignment. Distribution and personal services, the activities of a few in an agrarian world, become major economic roles in the society because, as a significant unit of consumption, the family does not by itself produce goods or services, nor has it access to the productivity of others. Increasingly, this state of affairs prevails even for those in agriculture. Large farm-factories relate a worker only to one crop, often one he cannot consume. He frequently lacks the traditional small holding for the raising of produce for his own family, the agricultural worker's wage supplement in transitional periods.

The complex requirements of modern productivity and citizenship demand a level of education well beyond the family's capacity to offer. Specialized institutions take over. Progress in science removes the primary group control over cure of illness. Similarly, the interdependence of modern urban life makes it dangerous for families to take the law into their own hands. Much of the internal protection and social control is socialized and becomes a responsibility of organized society. Some families desert the church in its role in guiding motivation and defining the desirable. Major affectional, child-rearing, socialization assignments are retained in the family, but even some of these give way as mothers of young children choose to or must work, marriages are broken by desertion or divorce, and adolescents pull away from family influence at young ages.

In the extended family, grandparents and other relatives were ever present to transmit norms and tradition, to guide and educate, to control. Now, given the physical mobility concomitant with industrialization, they may not be anywhere nearby. Even if close, they are less likely to be in the household—or, if there, are far less influential.

Husbands and wives themselves take advantage of formal educational and self-improvement activity or of the less formal, but commercially or socially organized, recreational-cultural activities that include bowling leagues, bridge and golf clubs, and garden clubs. Some devote time and effort to a diversity of civic activities. At the same time the usual neighborhood informal social activities may exist.

The above paragraphs are written as though there were only two family types today: remnants of the old-type extended family and modern, small, two-adult nuclear families. The 1970 White House Conference on Children reminded its participants that modern society is actually characterized by a diversity of family types: nuclear family, dyadic-nuclear family (childless, with at least one working), dual-work family, single-parent family, three-generation family, middle-aged or old-aged couple, kin network, second-career family, and institutional family. Emerging experimental and deviant structures include the monogamous commune family, the group-marriage commune family, the unmarried-couple-and-child family, and homosexual couples with adopted children.

Some of these are prevalent types, some relatively rare. Some are disapproved and others held up as models. But variations in family type are more common than the earlier ethic might have recognized. Children can and do flourish in many contexts—especially where there are social supports.[1]

What are the implications of all this: the decrease of familial functions in production, distribution, education, control, and so on; the multiplication of family "types" in the modern world; the elaboration of specialized functions in extrafamilial institutions, often large and remote; the breaking up of the extended family as a living unit; the assignment of some affectional primary group behavior to other institutions, while certain major responsibilities remain? Clearly, the answer is that unless the needs have disappeared—and they apparently have not—in the normal course of industrialization society must guarantee and institutionalize the means to assure that essential old functions are discharged in new ways and that new functions are recognized as legitimate response to new circumstances.

These, then, are the tasks of the social services:
1. To strengthen and repair family and individual functioning with reference to ongoing roles
2. To provide new institutional outlets for socialization, development, and assistance, roles that once were—but are no longer—discharged by the nuclear or extended family
3. To develop institutional forms for new activities, essential to individuals, families, and groups in the complex urban society even though unknown in a simple society

In other words, social services do not merely replace or seek to correct the family or earlier social forms. *They are also new responses to new social situations.* They are social inventions that seek to meet the needs of modern man in his interrelationships and roles, much as technical innovation is a response to the physical requirements of modern living.

Latent Functions

To consider social services in this way is to recognize how inadequate is the view that social services will no longer be needed as societies abolish poverty, increase equity, and cope with their current problems. Indeed, the very facts of economic growth and technological change depend upon and, in turn, stimulate major social changes. Such changes, we have seen, demand new institutional provision for meeting the affectional, socializational, developmental—as well as rehabilitative—needs of people. The very success of the economic growth process requires further institutional response. This is part of the purpose of social services. In short, the very process of implementation of concepts of fairness or equality requires institutional vehicles. The attack on old or new social problems—and new prosperity or economic forms do create new problems—also demands appropriate instruments.

Critics, particularly in countries that combine strong Puritan and pioneering strains with individualism (and this may include "socialist" states), attack the users of social services as in some way morally inadequate and as exploiters of the larger society. However correct this may be for the occasional malingerer, a universal if minority social role, it hardly characterizes the typical social service user in modern times. Indeed, "citizen" and "social service consumer" become synonymous terms in the industrial and post-industrial world.

There are others, often on the political left, who question social services as the "opium of the masses," a diversion from the "real problems" of achieving social equality and money and power redistribution. Social services, they allege, are "Band-Aids." The position has logical merit, but only from an anarchist's perspective. If society does not respond to change, does not adjust institutions to new needs, does not find new ways to enrich the lives of the young and the old—as old forms are outgrown—there may build up a pressure for social upheaval. He who believes that the continuation of adverse conditions is the road to social progress opposes social services. Others will agree that well-designed and effectively delivered social services may meet needs and may even create satisfactions. This is hardly a state of affairs to be avoided. Indeed, social services, on a substantial scale and of fundamental character, may signify and implement large-scale social change and societal enrichment. They may be the instruments for redistributional policy.

Even so, it remains true that at a given time or place one may discern that the latent intent of a particular proposal or program is to create a smoke screen, offer an illusion of solutions, divert political pressure. This kind of misuse is not rare in the political world: circuses rather than bread. A youth training program may be advertised with great fanfare to divert attention from the need for jobs. A major series of delinquency programs is launched to cover up the lack of an approach to adolescents who are at loose ends. A campaign is undertaken to train mothers to work and offer day care to their children as a way to obscure the refusal to develop an adequate income maintenance program for fatherless families. A request to fund a specialized counseling and group care program for blacks is approved as a way to avoid racial integration in a similar program nearby.

In short, there is no question that in the modern world social services perform essential, recognizable, even expanding functions. Their validity is unquestionable. Yet, proposals for a *given* service at a *given* time, and programs for implementing services in a specific way, merit scrutiny. The latent intent—usually relating to political strategies but sometimes otherwise motivated—may also be discerned and may shed light on issues of timing, focus, and program.

Not all latent functions reflect "plots" to divert and distort. In all public policy and action there is a multitude of motives and goals as actors join to promote or compromise on programs. With many unknowns in the equation, participants are often unable to anticipate fully what they have wrought or to perceive the functions discharged. Thus, some aspects of the Community Action Program, under the 1964 antipoverty war, may have been intended, by some of the designers, to "universalize" or "integrate" the civil rights movement, or to substitute a sociotherapeutic program strategy for a political approach. What occurred in some places, however, was different. An institutional base was offered and jobs became available more systematically to organize political and protest activity within the black community. On the other hand, paraprofessional jobs and money had the latent consequence of giving some people a stake in the status quo and co-opting them. The doctrine of participation spilled over into Model Cities and health programs with still other results, and launched other programs.[2]

Creating Social Integration

The approach up to this point would appear excessively utilitarian to some students of social policy. Whether they approach the matter from the tradition of religiously based charity or anthropologically informed social justice, there are observers who feel that it is not accurate to overemphasize the practical values of social services. To stress concrete socialization, care, support, and help—to the exclusion of all else—is to justify economizing and market approaches to policy choice, subjects which we discuss at a later point.

In a recent extraordinarily strong and dramatic statement, Richard M. Titmuss, the British social policy theoretician, argues that social policy is distinguished from economic policy because of its focus on institutions that "create integration and discourage alienation." Social services are involved in those areas of "personal behavior and relationships that lie outside the reciprocal rights and obligations of family and kinship in modern society." Social services encourage "anonymous helpfulness" and obligations that derive from one's own character, not from contracts.[3] Whether latent or manifest, altruism becomes a major function of social services in this sense—serving the donor as well as the recipient.

The Scope of Social Services in Differing Societies

It is useful to distinguish (a) those social services which become so elaborate and comprehensive as to achieve independent identity, and which in the United States are seldom thought of as social services (education, public [cash] assistance, medical care, public housing, especially), from (b) the remaining social services, encompassing a field with changing boundaries and including some "freestanding" programs (child welfare or family service agencies) and some that are located in other institutions (school social work, medical social service, social services in public housing, industrial social welfare programs, and so on).

The latter programs are the subject of this monograph. They may be described as "general social services." General social services are programs that protect or restore family life, help individuals cope with external or internalized problems, enhance development, and facilitate access through information, guidance, advocacy, and concrete help of several kinds.

To elaborate, a social service listing in a developing country might consider much of the above to belong to a subcategory called "social *welfare* services," insofar as they focus on assistance to individuals and families where there is a problem of adjustment and functioning or some deprivation to be remedied. A more inclusive "social service" list in such countries, addressing all population elements, would also include:

1. Social assistance (what Americans call public assistance or "relief")
2. Health programs (all those which are not private medicine)
3. Public education
4. All public housing activities
5. Manpower programs

Varying with the country, the list might or could include other activities ranging from recreational and cultural activity to public transportation, from area rehabilitation efforts to mass indoctrination as preparation for modernization.

Most industrialized countries yield social service listings whose scopes range between the United States illustrations presented above and the more inclusive listings of developing countries.* The main criterion seems to be the social decision to guarantee a program, a facility, a right because it is part of a communally conceived minimum or is believed to fulfill a broader public purpose so important that individual access should not be determined by adequacy or one's personal income and decisions made in the marketplace. While not rejecting these views, Titmuss also notes the job-market derivations of some services by describing them as compensation for socially caused diswelfare or as a substitute for salaries (occupational welfare).[4]

Definitions often refer to scope, purpose, or characteristics of the social services—or all three. For example, in the United Nations ". . . social service is defined as an organized activity that aims at helping toward a mutual adjustment of individuals and

---

*Recent British literature refers to the general social services (they use the term "personal" social services) as "the fifth social service," as distinguished from education, health, housing, income maintenance. See Peter Townsend, et al., *The Fifth Social Service* (London: Fabian Society, 1970).

Britain's relevant cabinet post, covering the Department of Health and Social Security, has jurisdiction over most general social services in our sense. It tends to concentrate a larger proportion of such services than does our own Department of Health, Education, and Welfare, which shares jurisdiction with a larger group of administrations, bureaus, and departments, despite its primary role. The responsible cabinet officer is known as the Secretary of State for Social Services.

their social environment. This objective is achieved through the use of techniques and methods that are designed to enable individuals, groups, and communities to meet their needs and solve their problems of adjustment to a changing pattern of society, and through cooperative action to improve economic and social conditions."[5]

A British report is somewhat similar in its perspective:

The social services cover a wide range of provisions to promote the health and well-being of the people of Britain and to improve the surroundings in which they live. The underlying motive is the recognition that the community as a whole has a responsibility to help its weaker and less fortunate members and to seek to secure for all its citizens those services which they cannot provide for themselves as individuals.[6]

In general, social services tend to be targeted on individuals, groups, and communities and to involve the rendering of help, the supplying of resources, and the implementation of benefits. The mutual aid and group targeting on broader social or economic conditions, described in the last phrase of the U.N. definition, is widely accepted conceptually but is actually not the common social service practice.

A United States task force suggested this:

Social services are those services rendered to individuals and families under societal auspices, excluding the major independent fields of service [that is, excluding health, education, housing, income maintenance].[7]

The following definition focuses on purposes:

Social services may be interpreted . . . as consisting of programs made available by other than market criteria to assure a basic level of health-education-welfare provision, to enhance communal living and individual functioning, to facilitate access to services and institutions generally, and to assist those in difficulty and need.[8]

The "other than market criteria" in this definition is important. It conveys a societal obligation or conviction about the importance of access to the benefit. Society has decided that an individual's inability to command a service in the marketplace—that is, his inability to pay for it out of earnings or wealth—should nonetheless not deprive him of it. Kenneth Boulding calls this a unilateral or nonreciprocated benefit, in the sense that the provider offers the service or goods whether or not the recipient is able to pay.[9]

Inevitably the range, quantity, and accessibility of social services will vary with a country's stage of development and wealth, and with the sociocultural and political factors that determine the priority accorded these claims upon national income. In the post-World War II period, for example, developing countries tended to give priority to those social services which might prepare people to assume employment in new industrial settings and to live in urban areas (literacy training and health services, for example).

As social services become more universally available and are more generally employed, for this is the tendency, there is a decreasing inclination to describe them as social *welfare* services, that is, services for those in need of *special* help and protection. On the other hand, these circumstances also create an increasing tendency to give subgroups of services independent institutional identities (health, education, housing, employment counseling) and not to refer to them as social services at all. It remains to be seen whether such processes will continue as the separation of most general social services from public financial aid (a subject to be discussed subsequently) becomes common practice in the United States, and as there is further recognition of the applicability of services, not to the poor alone, but to all population elements.

For the present, Willard Richan's summary is useful. He notes that social services may be seen as involving:

. . . a direct benefit, which is standardized for an identifiable population; it is socially sponsored, therefore accountable to the general society, and is exempted from (some of?) the rules of the marketplace.[10]

And we have added: While traditionally reserved for the disadvantaged and the troublesome, and thus describable as belonging to the class of social control mechanisms addressed to deviant groups, social services are increasingly recognized as applicable to the total population—or, more accurately, *some* social services are.

Human Services, Social Services, Social Welfare

Why is it that such fields as education or health may be included in a social services listing in one country and eliminated in another? An historical hypothesis may be offered.

Social work is a twentieth-century profession. However, since the breakup of feudalism there have existed rudimentary, often punitive, programs of care and control for the able-bodied poor, the elderly, dependent children, the handicapped, the mentally ill or retarded, the antisocial. They were long undifferentiated. The idea that the diverse kinds of programs we have listed be considered as components of a *system* of social services has developed within the past three or four decades. Much earlier the most industrialized and urbanized parts of the world had established extensive systems of public education and public health. These engendered their own professional hierarchies and their own organizational structures. They could not in fact be included in governmental administrative structures as components of a system that comprised child welfare, social (cash) assistance, family welfare, delinquency, and mental illness. They dwarfed these latter and refused to be associated with their stigma. For the fact that early social services had "poor law" derivations, and often implemented the controlling, punitive, or rehabilitative aspects of "last resort" public provision of funds for the families in dire economic need,[11] is part of the general social service legacy even today.

The notion that all who receive financial relief may be assumed to require personal guidance and rehabilitation has died hard. Nor has there been easy and immediate acceptance of the view that social services may have something to offer people who are not poor. Yet anyone could see that public education activities (and many could see that public health services) are valid for all.

Small wonder then that, in the United States, education and health were not included as "social services" and that other countries introduced the concept "social *welfare* services" specifically to identify programs for the needy and those in need of "help" rather than "service"—or those who are the objects of control or reform.

Great Britain and some other highly industrialized countries generally made the shift to a broad view after World War II, as "labor," "socialist," or "social justice" concepts led them to see

the relationships among the components: health, education, housing, employment services, child welfare, and so on. Developing
countries, beginning "near scratch," and with limited resources,
had no choice but to plan a comprehensive system with mutually
supportive components—even if distinguishing the provision for
all citizens from programs for the needy and sick. In the United
States we—and we are not alone—are not quite ready either to
see the whole or to ignore interrelationships completely. Rather,
we tend to develop new euphemisms to convey the concepts
implied in a broad view of social services. Increasingly, therefore,
one hears talk of "human services," which are, in effect, social
services, covering both universal services (services for all citizens) and those for groups in special need. Reference is also
made to "human resource programs," a less satisfactory term,
since it conveys the market-oriented notion of social services that
seek to prepare or rehabilitate people for manpower roles (see
page 95 re services as "investment") and does not encompass
other social service functions ("consumption").

What then is social *welfare*?* Social welfare as an institution
comprises all those policies and programs by which government
guarantees a defined minimum of social services, money, and
consumption rights, through the employment of access or distribution criteria other than those of the marketplace and through
demand management of the economy. All modern societies have
considerable social welfare commitment, and increasingly inter-
weave social welfare policies with economic, physical, tax, tariff,
transportation, and even broad political policies. It would therefore be conceptually accurate to describe the institution as "social
welfare," the services as "social services." For the reasons given
above, however, we may expect to confront for some time a distinction between social services and social *welfare* services—
and, perhaps, to discover a preference for some new term, such
as "human services."

Many professions and semiprofessions[12] are involved in social
services; such as, medicine, education, public recreation, physical
and vocational rehabilitation, nutrition, psychology, employment
counseling, and social work. Within the field that we have called
"general social services" (nonmedical, noneducational, and so

---

*In the United States, when the term "welfare" is used alone, it generally refers
to public (social) assistance programs (means-tested relief).

on), social work is the dominant, host profession. In recognition, general social services are now organized in Great Britain through local-authority social work departments. *Social work services* may thus be said to be those social services in which social work has a central role. They are sometimes rendered in agencies where social workers are the major group (family services or child welfare) and are sometimes adjunctive activities in schools, hospitals, residential institutions, or community agencies in which the social work service is less central to the main function. Historically, the majority of such services has been addressed to the poor, the troubled, the deviant, but services are increasingly being valued for broader population groups as well.

Socialist societies have tended to view social services in a somewhat different context. The concept of "public consumption" or "collective consumption" is employed to describe those goods and services that are, in other countries, both human services, in the above sense, and market-purchased items. The productivity and profit that might comprise the "wage pool" is deliberately divided on a policy basis, as between wages and public consumption. Reports note, for example, that several years ago public consumption in Romania represented an addition of 15.7 percent to real wages, whereas the U.S.S.R. stated that the increase was about one-third (these estimates are probably outdated, but the concept is of interest). The listing covers social services in the broadest sense as well as recreational and cultural items. The counseling-guidance-access service components are not very visible. The U.S.S.R. listing includes education, cultural activity, medical service, rest and convalescence, physical culture and sports, social insurance, social assistance, special programs for women, maternal and child care, aid to mothers of large families and to unmarried mothers, and housing (consumers pay only 4 to 5 percent of salaries for rent). Wages are paid according to labor-force factors, but public consumption goods are distributed regardless of the quality-quantity of an individual's work (what are called "non-market criteria").[13]

Because the socialist ideological and economic frameworks generate some policy issues of their own, this monograph will be relevant to those countries only insofar as issues and programming problems are shared by capitalist, mixed, and socialist societies. Indeed, since even within this field selection is essential for present purposes, the criterion of relevance to the U.S. *urban* scene will be applied constantly. For the most part, reference to other countries is made only where it clarifies elements germane to the primary focus.*

Can Social Services Expand?

This section introduces very briefly a subject that will appear on many agenda.

It has long been assumed that the post-industrial society, allocating increasing proportions of its labor force to the service—rather than the industry or agriculture—sections of the economy will continue to expand social (non-market) services. During the 1970s this assumption has been questioned in both Europe and the United States on the ground of costs. In simplified form, the new analysis goes as follows: Salaries and real income have continued to rise in both the private and the public sectors. In industry and agriculture the rationale has been a marked increase in productivity. (In fact, the Nixon new economic policy of 1972 permitted wage increases geared to productivity.)

However, salary increases in the public sector and in private social services have reflected unionization, political pressure, and concern for equity. The increased costs of services, coming at a time when citizens want more service and in the absence of increased productivity, have placed severe strains on government and on philanthropy. In some social service fields (hospital care) and in other parts of the public sector (sanitation), there is an all-out search for increased productivity. Elsewhere (counseling, advice, education, and so on), there is dispute as to the applicability of the concept. For the first time in some decades, even the most enthusiastic proponents of the social services have expressed uncertainty about future expansion.[14] For one thing, in the absence of rapid, new economic growth, government will lack the funds. For another, given the choice, consumers seem to prefer lower taxes and durable goods purchased in the market.

*There is considerable evidence of shared and parallel preoccupation with reference to social services in many countries. The records of the United Nations, UNICEF, and a number of other international bodies offer documentation, too, of shared endeavors pointed toward developing answers with some general validity.

The debate about economic growth, more generally, may also be relevant to the discussion. If the most pessimistic prophets of ecological disaster are right—we are writing in the midst of an unresolved debate—society must do more than curb its birthrates. Resources must be conserved and production must be decreased; otherwise, resource depletion, pollution, and overpopulation will overcome us. Planning under such circumstances will require considerable redistribution of resources in accord with social policy. But it will surely also be premised on a degree of service contraction or on careful selection of priorities and mix among social services. In either case, the specifics of social service policy will be of great importance.

And if the forecasts are wrong because new technology will correct pollution and substitute for depleted resources, the social and technological changes will create circumstances of great significance for the social services. Whatever response is given, it will need to be informed and considerable.

Typologies

Social services have been—and may be—classified in divers ways, depending on the purpose of the classification. For example, a United Nations publication concerned with the strategy of development planning considers the following to encompass the functions of social services:

1. The progressive improvement of the living conditions of people
2. The development of human resources
3. The orientation of people to social change and adjustment
4. The mobilization and creation of community resources for development purposes
5. The provision of institutional structures for the functioning of other organized services[15]

Apparent overlapping would appear to preclude use of such a listing for planning purposes.

Richard M. Titmuss, examining the manifest functions of social service from the perspective of the society, lists the following, which we have paraphrased, rearranged, and illustrated:

1. Services or benefits designed to add to the welfare of individ-

uals, families, or groups, immediately, or in the long run (a day-care program)

2. Services or benefits designed to protect society (probation)
3. Services or benefits designed as an investment in people essential to achievement of social goals (a manpower program)
4. Services or benefits designed "as compensation for socially caused disservices," where responsibility cannot be otherwise assigned (industrial accident compensation, compensatory programs where there has been racial discrimination) [16]

Of course one may also classify social services by program focus: occupational welfare, community service, school service, health-based service, institutional facilities, and so on.

As already noted, some countries distinguish between social services, the collective resources deemed essential for all citizens, and social *welfare* services, the programs designed for the needy and the unfortunate.

Martin Rein and S. M. Miller distinguish the following as the major current conceptions of the functions of social services: amenity, access, aid at transition points, and specialized alleviation.[17] While these authors tend to highlight differences among these several views of the functions of social services, we would argue that social services do have a series of important social functions that need not be seen in contradiction or conflict—even though different views are accented in competition for resources. For purposes of examining social services policy issues and problems related to the delivery of social services, the following classification of social service functions (which is illustrated below) is helpful and will be employed in this volume:

1. Socialization and development
2. Therapy, help, and rehabilitation (including social protection and substitute care)
3. Access, information, and advice

One might assume that these would always be identifiable, mutually exclusive functions, so that at any given moment all social services, such as those listed illustratively on page 30, would be easily classifiable. This is not the situation, however. From what has been already said, and from much yet to be introduced, it may noted that social services are at the heart of a society's value debates and political philosophies. How much and what should be guaranteed to all citizens? To what extent should a society urge citizens to rely on communal provision in contrast to individual initiative? What is the goal or emphasis of a given program? Are social services solely or largely for the unfortunate or the antisocial—or should there, under any circumstances, be a segregated system for such people? Should there be priorities for the poor or the deprived?

In this context, a given social service program may have different functions and different target populations within a given city, or under varied auspices. Sometimes a program form has varied possibilities and lends itself to sound use for different purposes; whether programs serving diverse groups and different objectives should be administratively separated or unified is a programming issue. Day care is generally a child development, socialization resource. However, a specialized day-care program may be therapeutically focused on a particular group of emotionally disturbed children. Or day care may be set up so that mothers will be compelled to work.

Similarly, homemakers may be a resource for all "normal" retired elderly in one place, or they may be employed to implement a rehabilitative program in another. Access or advocacy programs may be organized for universal usage or to help the very poor and deprived who are often closed out by many programs.

Despite these difficulties in subsuming ongoing programs under one category, and one category only, all the time, it will be useful for many of the purposes of the present undertaking to employ the threefold classification above.* Further elaboration and illustration is therefore in order.

SOCIAL SERVICES FOR SOCIALIZATION AND DEVELOPMENT

In a major sense, social services exist to protect, to change, or to innovate with respect to many of the educational, child-rearing, value-imparting, and social induction activities once assumed by the extended family, the neighborhood, and relatives. The goal is socialization into communal values, transmittal of goals and motivation, and enhancement of personal development. Cognitive and emotional aspects of learning are encompassed. The means are formal, semiformal, and informal.

---

*For many other purposes, as will be noted subsequently, a twofold classification also is helpful: social utilities and case services. See pages 76–84.

Among the relevant social services, even in countries that do not think of formal educational machinery and the activities of church groups as social services, are such things as:

1. Day-care or child development programs
2. Youth centers and hostels
3. Summer camping
4. Family planning
5. Lunch and breakfast programs in schools and churches
6. Centers for senior citizens
7. Home-delivered hot meals
8. Parent groups
9. Family vacation programs

SOCIAL SERVICES FOR THERAPY, HELP, REHABILITATION, AND SOCIAL PROTECTION

The phrase "substitute care" belongs in this title as well. Sometimes services seek to help individuals with problems by supplementing or substituting for the primary group supports, as in the instance of a Big Brother program or adoption. Often the focus is on brief, or intensive, personal help with environmental, situational, interpersonal, or intrapsychic programs. Frequently the goal is restoration of as much normal functioning as possible, where there is no real cure but the possibility of reasonable readjustment of relations between an individual or group and their social environment. Often the assignment is assuming societal control over "dangerous" or unacceptable deviance while help is rendered.

Included in this category are such services as:

1. Family casework services
2. Child welfare programs, particularly foster care and adoption
3. Probation and parole work
4. Group therapy
5. Friendly visiting of the handicapped or the aged
6. Therapeutic camps
7. Institutions for delinquents
8. Institutions for children in need of supervision
9. School social work with troubled or troublesome children
10. Medical social work
11. Child guidance programs
12. Protective services for the aging

ACCESS SERVICES

The need for social services focused on the access function has four sources: (1) Modern bureaucratic complexity, (2) variations among citizens in knowledge and understanding of rights or in appreciation of the values of certain resources, benefits, entitlements, (3) discrimination, and (4) geographic distance between people and services.

The incremental development of social services, the mixed motivations of their framers at various moments of history, and the sheer size of caseloads and staffs make it increasingly urgent that provision for access be made. Social workers as liaison personnel, "social brokers," "urban advocates," *assistantes sociales,* often devote their major efforts to spreading knowledge and creating linkages so that programs may be reached and used. In fact, the U.N.'s Third International Survey of social work education reported widespread acceptance of the following notion, one of the few universal characteristics of social work: "It is a liaison activity, through which disadvantaged individuals, families, and groups may tap all of the resources in the community available to meet their unsatisfied needs. . . ."[18]

The task of assuring access has become most urgent in recent decades, as program proliferation and increase of entitlement have not necessarily been followed by organizational realignment. Only an extremely well-informed citizen understands fully his rights and entitlements and the organizational machinery to be dealt with in gaining access to them.

Because the educated and the more affluent are more likely to know about or to have the ability to find out about services, there are those who would give priority to access services for the very poor. Others cite universal need. The question soon becomes enmeshed in all the issues relating to the universalism-selectivity policy, addressed in a later section. One specific form of the issue refers to the creation of special services for blacks, Indians, Puerto Ricans, Mexican Americans, and others who have suffered particular discrimination.

Access does not necessarily follow from provision of information alone. Access services may include information, advice, referral, complaints, case advocacy, class advocacy, and legal services, all on both individual and group bases. Included are such programs as neighborhood information centers, neighborhood legal services, "hot lines," ombudsman and complaint machinery, consumer education or self-protection groups, and radio and newspaper information services.

Brief mention may be made of an additional function sometimes attributed to social services: facilitating *participation*. A society faced by a history of exclusion and alienation may try to rectify long injustice and enhance local democracy by creating social services that encourage participation in community decision-making by the excluded. The Community Action Program under the U.S. antipoverty program, as launched in 1964, emphasized participation, as did the subsequent Model Cities program. In fact, the community organization method in social work, before it became increasingly preoccupied with formal planning, advocacy, and technical expertise in the late 1960s, was devoted overwhelmingly to facilitating citizen participation as volunteer direct service personnel, planners, fund raisers, and interpreters of programs. In the earlier period, however, the subjects of such programs were middle- and upper-middle-class Americans.

Recent participation programs have given special attention to the poor and to members of minority groups. Stress is placed on bringing citizens "indigenous" to a neighborhood into participation on all levels. The goal is variously seen as sociotherapeutic ("to reduce alienation"), individually therapeutic ("to give him a sense of confidence"), or political ("to redistribute resources and power").

Programs in this category include tenant organizations, special-interest action groups (welfare mothers), and volunteer recruitment services.

I have not included participation in the preferred typology, not out of failure to recognize the significance of participation as a goal, but because, in effect, it tends to overlap excessively with the other three categories. It represents a somewhat different classification perspective. Participation may be a *consequence* of how programs are organized, conducted and staffed—whether the primary or manifest objective is developmental, therapeutic, or the improvement of access.

Participation, in short, is sometimes means and sometimes goal, in my view. Nonetheless I recognize contrary perspectives. Kramer, for example, while quite realistic about limited successes and undesirable, unanticipated consequences, considers participation a category on a par with service. In fact, his well-documented case studies suggest that "participation" and "service" are two functions in tension and that choices must be made. In his words, the choice may have to be "the competent community or the competent program."[19] At least a given program may find it difficult simultaneously to promote both.

Nor have I suggested other possible principles of classification that, however valid, seem less fundamental than the distinctions among the three major service categories. For examples, (1) there are services targeted at individuals, at groups, and at institutions; (2) there are services that would control, change, or stabilize the deviant; and (3) there are "concrete" aids (food, shelter) and relationship-oriented assistance. Much will be said about these later in broader context, where they may be related to certain basic policy options.

NOTES

1. For this view see the report of Forum 14, *Report to the President, White House Conference on Children, 1970* (Washington: D.C.: Government Printing Office, 1971).
2. See articles by Sherry Arnstein, Melvin Mogulof, and Roland Warren in special section, "Planning and Citizen Participation," *Journal of the American Institute of Planners*, 35, 4 (July 1969).
3. Richard M. Titmuss, *The Blood Relationship* (New York: Pantheon, 1971), p. 212. The first phrase quoted is from Kenneth Boulding, "The Boundaries of Social Policy," *Social Work*, 12, 1 (January 1971), 7.
4. William A. Robson and Bernard Crick (eds.), *The Future of the Social Service* (Baltimore: Penguin, 1970), p. 15; and Richard M. Titmuss, *Essays on "The Welfare State"* (New Haven: Yale University Press, 1959), p. 50.
5. *The Development of National Social Service Programmes*, Report by a group of experts, sales no. 60.IV.1 (New York: United Nations Social Commission, 1959), p. 6.
6. Quoted from *Social Services in Britain* in United Nations, Department of Economic and Social Affairs, *Organization and Administration of Social Welfare Programmes: The United Kingdom of Great Britain and Northern Ireland,* sales no. 67.IV.6 (New York: United Nations: 1967), p. 1.
7. *Services for People,* U.S. Department of Health, Education, and Welfare (Washington, D.C.: The Department, 1968).
8. Alfred J. Kahn, *Theory and Practice of Social Planning* (New York: Russell Sage Foundation, 1969), p. 179.
9. Boulding, "The Boundaries of Social Policy," pp. 3–12.

10. Based on Willard Richan, "The Responsibilities of the Social Work Profession in the Delivery of Social Services," mimeographed (New York: National Association of Social Workers, 1968).

11. Blanche D. Coll, *Perspectives in Public Welfare* (Washington, D.C.: Government Printing Office, 1968); Karl de Schweinitz, *England's Road to Social Security*, Perpetua ed. (New Jersey: A. S. Barnes, 1961).

12. Amitai Etzioni (ed.), *The Semi-Professions and Their Organization* (New York: Free Press, 1969).

13. United Nations, Department of Economic and Social Affairs, *Organization and Administration of Social Welfare Programmes: The Union of Soviet Socialist Republics*, sales no. 67.IV.20 (New York: United Nations, 1967). Also, United Nations, Department of Economic and Social Affairs, *Organization and Administration of Social Welfare Programmes: Romania*, sales no. 67.IV.10, (New York: United Nations, 1967). The latter source, particularly, clarifies the notion that the services are expected to help individuals make a maximum contribution to productivity and, at the same time, to benefit from it. See pp. 1–4.

14. For interesting speculation, see S. M. Miller, editorial, *Trans-action*, October 1971; and Hugh Falk, "The Future Demand for Human Services," *New Generation*, Spring 1971.

15. United Nations, *Economic Bulletin for Latin America*, 11, 1 (April 1966), 79.

16. Richard M. Titmuss, "The Practical Case Against the Means-Test State," *New Statesman*, 74, 1905 (September 15, 1967), 308–310; and Vera Shlakman, "The Safety-Net Function in Public Assistance: A Cross National Exploration," *The Social Services Review*, 46, 2 (June 1972).

17. Personal correspondence.

18. United Nations, Department of Economic and Social Affairs, *Training for Social Work*, Third International Survey (New York: United Nations, 1958), p. 60.

19. Ralph M. Kramer, *Participation of the Poor* (Englewood Cliffs, N.J.: Prentice-Hall, 1969), p. 203.

What Services,
at What Costs?

Expenditures for general social services under the narrow definition here employed, are very modest: probably about 1 percent of
the gross national product (GNP), probably less than $10 billion
per year (1971), probably about $50 per capita. A full appreciation
of policy choices in this field requires some explanation of what is
included in these estimates and of the difficulty of accurate calcu-
lation. Such review also permits contrasting of the investment in
these programs with expenditures for income maintenance, medical care, education, and so on, and identification of choices that
may be involved in future allocations among programs.

Voluntary community fund raising for social welfare purposes in
the United States, by "community chests," "united funds," or the
like, often employs as a slogan some version of the following:
"Everybody Benefits—Everybody Gives."

The literal accuracy of the first part of the slogan will vary with

a number of factors. It is much more true if the social service listing includes developmental and socialization services (community
centers, Boy Scouts, and so on) than if limited to therapeutic or
"helping" programs. It is far more true if one refers to public
(statutory) programs such as elementary and secondary education,
than if consideration is limited to programs operated by voluntary
(private, nonstatutory) agencies and funded by the campaigns
alone. It is far more accurate if the intent is—and it generally is—
to include health programs (since considerable United Way funds
are allocated to voluntary hospitals serving entire communities)
that if limited to social services in the more common U.S. usage. In
short, United Way campaigns, while not necessarily using the term,
imply a broad, "European" definition of social services to include
health, recreation, and socialization (but not education or most
employment programs).

We may generalize loosely, but variations in definitions and
administrative auspices tend to complicate any effort to specify
statistically the participation in and utilization of programs or their
specific costs. The task is confounded further by the fragmentation
of responsibility within the public sector among departments,
among local-state-federal governments, and—within the voluntary
sector—among many sectarian and nonsectarian bodies. Even
where the social bookkeeping may be competently organized and
adequately backed, aggregated data are not easily subdivided, and
fragmented data can seldom be aggregated to yield useful totals
and rates. Under these circumstances it is difficult to talk about
caseloads and costs in satisfactory fashion. Nor is it possible to
report either expenditures or users under categories resembling
our general social services subclassifications: development-socialization, help-treatment, access.

Were we to limit our social services definition to social insurance and related programs, generalization about users and price
would be easy: virtually all people currently in the labor force are
participating, before long almost all persons will have some
entitlement at the point of retirement, and almost all dependent
survivors of deceased people will have some benefits. Similarly,
elementary and secondary public schooling or acceptable private
alternatives are universal, and there are known rates for college
attendance. Costs are reported. Health statistics, referring both to
outpatient medical care and hospitalization, are more difficult to
aggregate; but useful surveys exist. Public and some private costs
are known. However, as indicated, our focus—following U.S. prac-

tice—is upon general social services *excluding* income security, health, education, housing, and general employment services.

What are the costs? What part of *all social service* costs (broad definition) are allocated to *general social services* (in our sense)? And how many Americans are service utilizers in various programs?

Costs

The comprehensive survey, *Social Welfare Expenditures Under Public Programs in the United States, 1929–66*,[1] defines social welfare very broadly. It permits identification of three categories relevant to a focus on social services narrowly defined as well, however: "other social welfare," "other public aid," and "veterans' programs." The first encompasses vocational rehabilitation (much of which is medical), federal-state-local institutional care, school meals, child welfare services, special antipoverty programs, and some programs not otherwise classified. "Other public aid" includes refugee aid, commodity and food stamp programs and the antipoverty job programs. The overall veterans' category is devoted largely to income, education, and health programs, but it also covers federal and state "welfare and other" activities. Among the latter are subsumed domiciliary care, beneficiary travel costs, vocational rehabilitation, counseling, automobiles for the disabled, specially adapted homes, information services. (Some administrative costs are included.)

In fiscal 1970–1971 the public social welfare expenditure total was 16.9 percent of the gross national product, or $170.8 billion (social insurance and other public income maintenance accounts for $66.0 billion of this total and education for $55.5 billion) in a year when the GNP was $1050.4 billion. The $170.8 billion constituted almost half of all American governmental expenditures. The private social welfare expenditure total for 1970–1971 was $72.3 billion, contributing to a grand total of $239.8 billion for social welfare (social services broadly defined), or 23 percent of the GNP.

General social services in the *narrower* sense of this monograph, in so far as they are identifiable under the subcategories listed above and separable from administrative costs, probably accounted for $10 billion of public plus voluntary expenditures in 1970–1971, of which 85 percent were public (see Table 1). The major public general social service programs were work experience, food stamps, surplus food, school meals, institutional care, child welfare, special antipoverty programs, veterans welfare services, and vocational rehabilitation. (Data in this part subject to small corrections following later tabulations. *Social Security Bulletin,* December, 1972 now specifies $950,000 for public assistance services—a total previously commingled with administrative costs. Most general social services will show increases for 1971–72.)

The private "welfare and other services" category, including settlement houses, family service agencies, child welfare, programs for the aged, institutional care of many kinds, church social services, and so on, is estimated at between $1.5 and $2.0 billion.

The $10 billion overall expenditure, perhaps an overstatement, particularly as regards private totals, is also seen in perspective if recognized as constituting only slightly more than 1 percent of the GNP. General social services obviously is not the social service component (using the broader definition) now representing the major U.S. investment. Note the following:

Table 1 General Social Services Expenditures (Public) 1969–1970 and 1970–1971

Program and Administrative Expenditures	1969–1970 (In thousands)	1970–1971 (In thousands)
"OTHER PUBLIC AID"	$2,042,388	$3,187,249
Surplus commodities	289,423	313,000
Food stamps	576,884	1,573,000
Refugee assistance	59,619	76,340
OEO and manpower[a]	1,116,462	1,224,903
"WELFARE AND OTHER" (federal, state and local veteran programs)[b]	$ 319,703	$ 367,597
"OTHER SOCIAL WELFARE"	$4,606,052	$5,305,093
Vocational rehabilitation[c]	699,074	790,337
Institutional care	1,582,453	1,759,000
Child nutrition[d]	895,988	1,214,944
Child welfare services	509,697	504,817
Special antipoverty programs[e]	752,800	786,200
Not elsewhere classified (federal)[f]	166,040	249,795
GRAND TOTAL	$6,968,143	$8,859,939
Minus medical services and medical research under vocational rehabilitation	$6,804,741	$8,680,730

[a]Includes Job Corps, in-school work support, work experience programs, private-sector on-the-job training, public-sector on-the-job training, post-school work

Table 2 Social Welfare Expenditures as Percentage of U.S. Gross National Product, 1970–1971[a]

Income maintenance		8.8
Health		7.4
Education		6.8
Welfare and other services		1.2
	Total	24.2

[a]These data are from the Office of Research and Statistics, Social Security Administration. My estimate of 1.0 percent for general social services reflects a somewhat narrower definition than "welfare" in the sense of the above table.

As will be noted in Table 1, the "other social welfare" is a major component of public social services (and it is probably even larger, proportionately, in private agency services). Available HEW series indicate that such services now account for .5 percent of GNP. Modest as this may be, when contrasted with income maintenance, health, or education, it is a fivefold increase since 1928–1929 (from .1 percent) and over 60 percent increase since the 1960s (from .3 percent).

Is 1.0 percent of GNP a significant figure for general social serv-

---

support and related programs. MDTA education, training allowances, and employment services not included.

[b]For 1970–1971 the administrative component in the federal total was $176,522,-000 out of $277,597,000 federal expenditure. This covers unallocated administrative costs for all veterans' programs. Totals include domiciliary care, beneficiaries' travel, vocational rehabilitation for veterans; also counseling, special autos, homes, and lifts for disabled veterans.

[c]Largely a federal program; a significant component of the expenditure is for *medical* service and research. This component is deleted, where readily identified, from the overall total, as indicated subsequently.

[d]Includes school lunches, school breakfasts, and related programs.

[e]Includes community action operations, migrant work programs, VISTA, health and nutrition programs, legal services, other, administration.

[f]Indian welfare and guidance activities; aging activities; HEW secretary; juvenile delinquency programs; Cuban refugee resettlement. Cooperative research in social security; administration of certain manpower activities; Social and Rehabilitation Service (SRS) salaries and expenses; specified research and training projects in SRS.

SOURCE: Office of Research and Statistics, Social Security Administration. The interpretation and arrangement is mine. "Other public aid" is all federal expenditures. Public expenditures in the other two categories are also state and local.

ices? The per capita figure (about $50) is, of course, comparatively
high as an absolute sum, given our high national income compared
with that of other countries. However, while relatively, but not
precisely, comparable categories of service apparently command a
smaller percentage of GNP in some of the western and northern
European industrial countries and slightly higher percentages in
others, only a major, new, international effort could produce truly
comparable computations for detailed analyses. For present purposes we note that, whatever the relative size of the investment, it
is small in absolute terms. Counseling interviews may cost
$20–$25 per hour, testing just as much, home helpers $20–$30 per
day, shelter $55–$65 per day, training schools for delinquents
$5,700 per year (but $8,760 in the North Pacific area), residential
treatment $12,000–$18,000 per year, modest day care $2,000 per
year—and so on.*

We could, with Miller and Altschuler, add to these totals items
for the employment services in federal and state government (the
issue is debatable, but the case is good), all vocational-technical
training and adult education (which would seem to belong with
education), and other rehabilitation items (which may be substantially medical). The U.S. Office of Management and Budget, for
example, reports 1971 manpower expenditures as $3.1 billion and
1972 estimated expenditures as $4.3 billion. For the present pur-
poses, some notion of scale is suggested by the rough total of
$10.0 billion for the items we have included, a per capita annual
expenditure of some $50 for 1971, and the evidence of very sub-
stantial growth even in comparison with much else in social
welfare in recent years.[2]

In the "other social welfare" category, for 1970–1971 the state-
local share was over $2.5 billion and the federal over $2.7 billion.
The federal share, under 40 percent of the total in 1965, continues
to grow. The federal costs are highest for child nutrition, special

---

*In New York State, in 1972, the median inpatient costs in a children's state hos-
pital for the mentally ill was $8,700, but one private treatment agency ran up
annual per capita costs of $31,200. Average costs in state training schools for
delinquents in New York for that year ranged from $8,137 to $17,046. Voluntary
institutions for the retarded reported per capita costs of $14,400, whereas state
schools spent $3,220–$3,650 (to which one might add capita costs of $4,000 per
capita.) See *Juvenile Justice Confounded: Pretensions and Realities of Treatment Services*, Report of the Committee on Mental Health Services Inside and
Outside the Family Court in the City of New York (Paramus, N.J.: National Council in Crime and Delinquency, 1971).

OEO programs, and vocational rehabilitation, in that order. Major state costs are for institutional care and child welfare. The relevant veterans' programs, as indicated, are largely federal. The "other public aid" expenditures are by definition federal.

When health, education, income maintenance, and the more narrowly-defined general social services are combined, the public/private ratio is 70:30. The federal/state-local ratio is 54:46. Private expenditures are most important in health (about 62 percent of the total) and are small in all other social welfare categories, including general social services (under 25 percent).

This public-voluntary distribution may very well be changed at the point of service delivery, since public funds are increasingly expended through nonstatutory or semipublic programs. To illustrate: The federal government expended at the rate of $1.6 billion for social services under the Social Security Act in 1972. Of the sum, one-third was for purchase of care through the voluntary sector or other public programs.*

Programs and Users

If they are systematically reported at all, operational statistics usually refer to specific agencies and programs. They are often meant for promotional purposes, to impress budget makers (public) or contributors (voluntary). They certainly cannot be aggregated. Individual community surveys may remedy these defects but employ their own definitions or are narrower in focus. Occasional national surveys have been made, but none seeking user estimates for general social service specifically. If one had to make a very rough "best guess" on the basis of extrapolations, it would be that half of all "case" services—services to help, treat, or rehabilitate—are utilized by about 6 percent of the families in

---

*A significant expenditures increase took place in 1972 under automatic matching formulae in Title IV–A of the Social Security Act before Congress closed the "open end" matching. States had become quite inventive in qualifying their "normal" expenditures as the state matching funds; in this way each state dollar generated three federal dollars. A movement to end this practice developed but was opposed by those who defined it as an unintended form of revenue sharing. As we went to press it was not possible to discern the effects of the "closing" of the "open end" in the expenditures trends we have outlined. (Note: Some items in the $1.6 billion do not qualify as general social services under our definition.)

an urban population at a given time. The other half are more broadly distributed. No comparable estimate is possible with reference to developmental programs or access services—or for locations other than large cities—and the estimate given would hardly survive close scrutiny.

What follows takes a national perspective. It is offered only for *orientation* purposes, and to specify what some of the general social service programs actually are. I refer to agencies, programs, caseloads, staffs—but all in a limited way.[3] At most, the generalizations are in the locus of the facts but should not be deemed precise or appropriately qualified. In a *given* context, policy development or programming would require assembling considerable data about users.

Many of the concrete services referred to under expenditures cannot be here described in terms of users. There are few and vague consumer statistics. On the other hand, social service planners report more detail on relationship and substitute-care services. These categories of services tend to be recorded, since they have long been the focus of social work agencies. As the following materials about limited users of case services are considered, therefore, it may be useful to recall that in 1971 some 10.5 million people participated in food stamp programs and 3.0 million received surplus food commodities. In 1969 3.0 million children were receiving free or below-cost school lunches. The total rose to 6.6 million in 1971, and by early 1972 the total was over 8.0 million. There were over 11.0 million recipients of Aid to Families with Dependent Children (AFDC) in 1972, some 8.0 million of whom were children.*

PERSONAL AND FAMILY COUNSELING

In theory, many millions of public assistance recipients in categories other than AFDC (aged, blind, handicapped, and so on) have had access to counseling, help, referral, and various related concrete social services. As a matter of fact, most public assistance investigators (or "social workers," as they may be called)

---

*Although there is no measure of service depth or content, the National Center for Social Statistics summarizes state reports as indicating the following general social service rates for AFDC cases: 41 percent receive counseling, guidance, and so on; 24 percent are referred for work or training; and 8 percent receive vocational rehabilitation.

have had to concentrate on eligibility and employment issues. Few of them were qualified for more than generalized "friendly visiting," if accepted by their clients in, and if they found time for, a personal helping role.* At this writing a process is under way to separate the eligibility investigation administratively from the social service function. It is this very process that gives immediacy to some of the policy and program issues discussed subsequently in this volume.

Within veteran programs some 2,000 social workers and related personnel render individual and group counseling services. An unknown proportion of vocational rehabilitation funds and of medical costs is also devoted to counseling.

Relative to population size, the population at large has access to a small amount of private psychiatric and marriage counseling, and to service by some 340 family service agencies, rendering help of varied intensity to some 150,000 families a year (following screening or referral of about another 300,000 cases). The latter agencies tend to be staffed by trained social caseworkers (about 2,500).

Counseling within the armed forces and by religious counselors, church-related social service programs, and many group programs are not here included. Nor can we estimate the exact extent to which school-based social workers, hospital-based medical and psychiatric social workers, union and industry social workers, psychiatrists, or psychologists go beyond the helping situation that arises in the special setting to engage in a broader casework, counseling, or psychotherapeutic process. It is now expected that general hospitals, medical clinics, psychiatric hospitals, schools, community centers, and camps will offer special casework help to those whose situations call for assistance in utilizing the basic service and—perhaps—to those revealed to have personal problems impeding general adjustment. Some of these facilities, especially hospitals, have facilitators or complaint adjusters, often erroneously called "ombudsmen." Many of the thousands of

---

*Joel Handler found in his Wisconsin study very little direct service in public welfare, despite the intensive efforts to free public assistance workers for a casework role in the 1950s and early 1960s. See Joel Handler and Ellen Jane Hollingsworth, "The Administration of Social Services and the Structure of Dependency: The Views of AFDC Recipients," *The Social Service Review*, 43, 4 (December 1969), 406–420. Or the same authors, *The "Deserving Poor": A Study of Welfare Administration* (Chicago: Markham Publishing Co., 1971).

trained social workers in these agencies are engaged in casework services that may be described as intensive. Beyond this, in the general category of home or community care, or aftercare, many thousands of aged or mentally ill or defective or addicted or adjudicated or handicapped individuals are sustained through daily difficulties and given access to concrete services and resources by virtue of the activities of social workers (or counselors from related disciplines) affiliated with a diversity of institutional auspices. Protective services are becoming increasingly important for the aged who live in the community and may need outside intervention to avoid their exploitation or harm.

Over 900 antipoverty neighborhood centers are also the location of some social services. Counseling may be rendered by various categories of personnel, at levels of training ranging from the M.D. psychiatrist, the Ph.D. or M.A. psychologist, and the M.S. social worker, on the one hand, to the grade-school-educated local person with "instinct" and background for helping his neighbors. Caseload estimates do not exist. The service rendered ranges from sporadic "advice" or "information" to intensive personal help.

CHILD WELFARE

Foster home care, adoption services, institutional care for children, and temporary shelter during familial emergency constitute basic social services. They have existed as long as social services have been known, and have a history in the United States going back to the eighteenth century, even if we discount indenture and other precursors. The Department of Health, Education, and Welfare estimates that early in 1970 some 3 million different children received some social services from public or voluntary agencies specializing in child welfare or incorporating child welfare responsibilities. Most of the service was in public programs.[4]

A relatively complete institutional census conducted in 1966 showed the following: 60,500 children in 955 institutions for the dependent and neglected (children without families or in danger from their families); 55,000 in 414 institutions meant for the adjudicated or adjudicable delinquent; 13,900 in 307 institutions for the emotionally disturbed; 8,000 in 145 psychiatric inpatient units; 6,000 in 201 maternity homes; 1,800 in 54 temporary shelters awaiting plans or facilities; and 10,900 in 242 more secure (detention) facilities awaiting court dispositions or facilities.

Left out of the census because of jurisdictional issues were 701 facilities for mentally retarded children and 373 for the physically handicapped. The child total was about 165,000–170,000 for the institutions studied and approximately 100,000 for the others; the 1972 grand total estimate for institutionalized children is 250,000.

In addition, 175,000 were adopted in 1970, about half by non-relatives. (Of the 175,000 about 110,000 adoptees were born out of wedlock.) Three-quarters of the nonrelative adoptions were served by social agencies, whereas social agencies served only a few of the relative adoptions.

Furthermore, several hundred thousand children have exposure to social services of various degrees of intensity and competence rendered by probation officers and court intake departments. Smaller numbers are helped by trained juvenile police in special juvenile aid bureaus. Many are held in jail detention with no service at all. Between 150,000–200,000 cases of dependent and neglected children may have some exposure to court social services annually as well (over 133,000 such cases were processed and recorded in 1970). And of some 91,000 children under eighteen who were psychiatric inpatients in 1969 in general hospitals, state and county mental hospitals, residential treatment centers, community mental health centers, and private mental hospitals, some did and many did not have social service help. For example, the 261 residential treatment centers, perhaps offering the most intensive service, employed 1,630 social workers and some 700 counselors for coverage to patients occupying about 15,000 beds (psychiatrists, psychologists, teachers not here included). We have no data at all about social services to the some 600,000 children who were psychiatric outpatients at the same time.

These totals should be related to a base of 45 to 65 million children, age eligibility for the several programs varying.

Of the children served by public child welfare services other than adoption, over a third are the victims of parental neglect or abuse. Close to one-fifth require help because they are uncared for in time of parental death, illness, or desertion. Some are deemed out of control, or too disturbed to function normally. Voluntary child welfare services tend to concentrate on cases involving parent-child relationship problems (also a major preoccupation in the family counseling cases mentioned above) or out-of-wedlock births. The services are both concrete and practical (finding a foster home, arranging for a homemaker) and counseling (coping with separation, helping one adjust to a new home). About 4,000 agencies are involved, half of them institutions.

The situation is summarized as follows:

Table 3 Children Receiving Social Services from State and Local Public Welfare Agencies, and from Voluntary Agencies, March, 1970[a]

Location of Service	State and Local Public Agencies	Voluntary Agencies and Institutions
Served while "at home"	2,397,000	44,000
In independent living arrangements	10,500	4,800
In foster family homes	243,000	41,300
In group homes	3,500	2,500
In institutional care	63,100	63,300
In adoptive homes	42,700	37,900
Elsewhere	8,000	2,100

[a]To age twenty-one in some jurisdictions. Combines AFDC and "child welfare" cases. Service ranges from token "coverage" to intensive "treatment." There are 59,600 cases, which appear among both the public and voluntary subcategories. The unduplicated total is 2,909,000.

SOURCE: National Center for Social Statistics, Department of Health, Education, and Welfare, Report E-9 (March 1970).

There are full-time publicly employed child welfare workers in all but a small number of U.S. counties today; nationally they total over 15,000. Almost every county now has some coverage, even if part-time or private. Many counties consider themselves under-staffed, however. Community and institution-based child care-workers constitute a labor force of approximately 100,000. Most are "pre-" or "sub-" professional.

Although part of day care and Head Start or nursery programs is categorized as in the province of education, and much of the expenditure is tabulated as education under federal expenditure studies, these kinds of child care may be seen as a developmental-socialization social service. Most standard-setting groups see child care as a social service conducted jointly by educators, social workers, doctors, and related professionals. In addition to educational components, good programs are expected to include (or assure access to) social service, health, nutrition, and parent participation components.

There are currently (1971) 26 million children under fourteen years old with working mothers in the United States, of whom 6 million are under six years of age. Of these about 700,000 are in licensed group and family day care. Of the total of 1.3 million children in care, some 600,000 are in centers and over 710,000 in homes. Most of the centers are licensed; most of the homes are not. About half of the group care is proprietary. Some 200,000 children are in programs financed under the assistance titles of the Social Security Act, under child welfare, and under "work incentive" programs (Title IV–A is the major funding source). About 100,000 are in all-day Head Start programs, a development out of the antipoverty effort. Other children participate in before- and after-school programs. Most of these children are cared for by friends, relatives, siblings, or an unrelated neighbor while their mothers work. Much expansion in publicly sponsored care is projected or is currently under way in an effort to free more welfare mothers to work or to provide better care in the thousands of instances where working mothers are concerned about poor arrangements.[5] In this, too, several issues reside.

THE AGED

Some of the counseling services described above reach the aged. About 8 percent of all older people are served in community centers or settlement houses with recreation and other leisure-time group services. Others are in medically-based nursing homes. Of some 20 million persons over sixty-five, about 4 percent, or 850,000, live in institutions of some kind. The aged in the community receive uncounted "concrete" and counseling services. Others in hospitals, geriatric facilities, and psychiatric programs are under medical care, also supplemented by general social services. Special apartments for the aged, as well as buildings, housing developments, or camps for them, often have supplementary general social services. Homemaker and home-help programs, major social service resources for the aged in some other countries, often as rights under social insurance, are thus far little developed in the United States. Modest medically-based home care equivalents, provided under Medicare, are expanding. Similarly, protective services for the aged, "meals-on-wheels," and friendly visiting, basic social services in some places, are relatively rare in the United States. Given the size of the group and its population proportion, expansion in all these realms is projected.

ADJUNCTIVE SOCIAL SERVICES

Although there are debates about specific functions, social services—usually manned by professionally trained social workers—
are located in or sought by schools, general hospitals, and psychiatric facilities in the United States. In foreign countries they are
common in industry, an infrequent occurrence in the United States.
In some places they are sponsored by or located in labor unions,
not the typical U.S. pattern despite considerable activity during
World War II and some recent expansion.[6] These social workers
focus on practical difficulties (illness of a spouse, for example) or
personal problems (such as extreme anxiety) or interpersonal con-
flicts (like trouble with a former spouse) that interfere with a person's ability to meet responsibilities or use resources adequately.

It is generally agreed that in settings such as these the social
services are adjunctive, that is, they are supportive of the primary
mission of the host institution and of the individual's utilization of
the core service (education, psychiatry, general medicine, and so
on) or his functioning in his relevant role (worker, student, union
member). However, social workers and aides in such social service programs also may conceive of themselves as carrying some
responsibility to participate in defining the core policies of schools
and hospitals as institutions and as contributing to organizational
renewal. They also are in varying degrees preoccupied with the
total well-being of the individual, even if it means not giving
primacy to his role performance. Professional ethics at certain
points dictate protection, and even withdrawal, of a sick client in
the face of unmanageable demands by a school, for example. Certain obvious problems in professional ethics follow.

General medical and psychiatric facilities that emphasize community care as a substitute for or as a rapid follow-up to the time
spent in the institution place considerable emphasis on the role
of social workers and others as adjunctive to the medical specialty. Day and night hospitals and various part-institutionalization
programs, involving a segment of the day spent in a protected
setting, also emphasize the general social service, as contrasted
with the specific medical component.

ADVOCACY AND LEGAL SERVICES

Legal aid and neighborhood legal services have been recognized in
recent years as having a major role in assuring access to public
housing, income maintenance programs, and similiar public pro-

grams. They of course also have central, major, specifically legal functions, entering into cases relevant to a specific individual's interests, as well as cases that "make" new law and policy affecting total classes of situations. There are (1972) approximately 2,200 lawyers operating out of 850 storefronts in 250 cities under the antipoverty program, and also a significant number of other legal aid units dealing with civil cases.

VOCATIONAL REHABILITATION

While it is virtually impossible completely to separate what are basically medical programs from those in which general social services are a major component, it may be noted that professional practice in this field gives high priority to the role of the vocational counselor as a "coordinator" of the specialities as they are addressed to the particular case. He also carries responsibility for continuity of the care and for following outcomes. Social workers may play such roles, too, or may have some specialized tasks in rehabilitation. There are some 8,500 facilities and workshops that define themselves as "rehabilitative" in the United States.

HOMEMAKERS AND HOME HELPS

It is estimated (1971) that there are 17,000–22,000 home-health aides and homemakers in the United States serving child welfare, the aged, and medical and family service programs. In 1965 the British total was 30,000. The U.S. ratio of 1:10,000 population, therefore, compares with 1:1,700–1,800 people for England.

There are no comparable meals-on-wheels statistics. The program is so small in the United States as to make ratios meaningless. It has significant British and Scandinavian development.

COMMUNITY CENTERS, SETTLEMENTS, AND GROUP PROGRAMS

YMCAs, boys' clubs, sectarian and nonsectarian community centers (public and voluntary) for several or for all age groups, Aspira clubs for Puerto Rican children, settlement houses, scouting programs, Campfire Girls, Girl Guides, local group programs under religious-nonsectarian-service-charitable organizations, and other related groups serve millions of people. They combine character development, child development, talent encouragement, socialization, educational, camping, recreational and therapeutic compon-

ents in various proportions.* The core professional skills involved
are social work (group work), education, physical training, and
recreation. Many volunteer leaders and college students serve
these programs.

It is virtually impossible to include estimates of participation in
or even of units offering programs of educational-cultural enrichment under divers auspices.

FAMILY PLANNING

Here the core professional skill is medical. Large numbers of
social workers are also needed because of the promotional-edu-
cational, family relationship, personal adjustment, and management aspects of the effort. Services are increasing so rapidly in
hospitals, Planned Parenthood centers, neighborhood health centers, and related facilities as to outdate available statistics. Social services are also rapidly expanding in connection with abortion clinics and hospital abortion services, as state laws are lib-
eralized. And hundreds of thousands of young people are enrolled
in family life courses in schools, churches, and community centers.

JOB PLACEMENT AND TRAINING

Auspices are provided by official state and city programs, several
federal manpower programs, local antipoverty units, educational
facilities, veteran and rehabilitation programs, and medical facilities, among others. It has been estimated that in fiscal 1971 federal programs alone, with some degree of participation by millions
of people, cost over $3 billion. Almost 566,000 were in Labor
Department sponsored programs.[7] Staffing of these programs is by
job placement specialists, vocational and basic educators, psychologists and testers, group counselors, and a quite limited
number of social workers and others who focus on problems
of adjustment, participation, and personal counseling. In our
sense, the latter are the general social service concerns. Recent emphasis on "workfare," the tying of public assistance
eligibility to participation in public works, public employment,

*The National Federation of Settlements has some 350 centers; there are some
450 Jewish Community Centers and Ys. Four youth-serving organizations (4-H,
Boy Scouts, Girl Scouts, Campfire Girls) reported 11 million members in 1970.

counseling, and training programs, by those unemployed and deemed employable, is rapidly expanding the social service component in manpower programs. Boundaries between labor-market placement programs and programs that may be considered to belong in the social service family remain vague.

PARTICIPATION

There is no estimate of service "volume" in this vague category. Included are a diversity of programs under antipoverty Community Action, based in at least 1,000 centers; policy-advisory-planning committees or groups in 150 Model Cities programs; many state and regional planning enterprises under "partnership-for-health" amendments; some local participation in advising or planning community mental health centers; various types of local participation in, or reaction to planning in, urban renewal, public housing, highway programs, and local multiservice centers under several programs; tenant organization; new forms of community "control" or participation in urban ghetto schools; local organization under settlement house auspices; a diversity of other programs related to self-help or the search for political power by deprived ethnic minorities; and so on. Some of these programs are professionally or subprofessionally staffed by community organization or community development personnel; some are truly locally controlled; and some are neither staffed nor truly autonomous. Some see participation sociotherapeutically, some politically. To some it is window dressing.[8]

Personnel

The broad definition of social services implies recognition that a variety of disciplines and professions may be involved in any given program. As we have narrowed the field, separating education, health, and housing, we have eliminated programs in which educators, doctors, nurses, and architects are the primary movers, while noting that some general social service components may be related to their efforts.

The more restrictive definition of general social services constitutes it as a field in which—with some exceptions—social workers are the core or "host" profession. The major exceptions occur in employment, in group-community center activities, and in family planning. Of course, as already indicated, even in fields like child welfare and family counseling, there are major interdisciplinary aspects.

To estimate the nonsocial work component in each of the general social service areas would be tedious, inaccurate, and relatively pointless. It is more productive to orient the discussion to basic policy questions and to issues of program strategy by an overview of the social work manpower situation, since this is the core on which one must build.

There are currently almost 14,000 full-time graduate students enrolled in the two-year M.S. program. For lack of an up-to-date survey that includes M.S.-holding social workers, those trained at the baccalaureate level, and the many "noncredentialed" aides who have appeared in large numbers, particularly under the impetus of the antipoverty program, we are compelled to cite the following estimates:

about 150,000 M.S. and B.A. social workers of whom 53,000 are part of the professional association, National Association of Social Workers; over 2,000 vocational rehabilitation counselors; and 170,000 "noncredentialed" antipoverty aides, many of whom are not full-time.*

Apart from the antipoverty aides, two-thirds or three-quarters of the social workers are probably in public programs and the remainder in voluntary. The public social work staffs concentrate in public assistance and child welfare. From the point of view of policy planners the issues are the training levels essential for different functions, the organizational patterns for interrelating personnel with different types of credentials, the suitability of current training for new modalities of service, and the core professional discipline for the training of certain categories of personnel.

Social services have, traditionally, engaged large numbers of volunteers in the United States; in fact, early social service pro-

*Early in 1970 it was estimated that in antipoverty community action programs alone there were 91,000 people with credentials from the several professions (social work, education, law, counseling, physical education, and so on). The social work total includes many institutional child-care personnel.

grams were manned completely by volunteers until late in the nineteenth century,[9] when professionalization began. The American ethic has, from the beginning, valued voluntary good works, and millions of citizens are willing to serve their fellows who are under stress and have special needs. Hospital "gray ladies" and "candy stripers" are universal phenomena. Reading tutors, escorts who take aged citizens to clinics, and "friendly visitors" to institutions serve in many places. Peace Corps and Vista volunteers and members of the Teachers Corps have become widely known in recent decades. A federal agency known as Action, created in 1971, unifies them.

Volunteer efforts other than fund raising may be classified to distinguish among (a) assistance to others ("case" services), (b) mutual aid, and (c) social action and class advocacy. Because definitions are loose and comprehensive data nonexistent, it is impossible to say whether the use of paid social service staffs has been accompanied by a decline in voluntary service. A White House-endorsed National Center for Voluntary Action, cooperating with the governmental Action program, is seeking to recruit even more volunteers and to broaden the range of their concerns.[10]

Social service agencies everywhere, whether operated under public or private auspices, deal constantly with the question of which services are appropriately conducted by volunteers and which by paid staff—and how personnel in the two categories may interrelate. If the 1950s was an era of high professionalization and constriction of volunteer opportunity, and the 1960s a period of expansion of paraprofessionals and of offering the poor job opportunities in the social services, the 1970s would appear to be a time when an effort is under way to restore volunteering to a more central place in social services. It is not clear whether such efforts will succeed in a context of large-scale organization—and when people are seeking paid social service jobs. Nonetheless, extensive voluntarism seems likely to continue on the scene in the predictable future.* It has been estimated that as many as 30 to 50 million Americans volunteer now during a given year, although such totals include many people whose activity is quite limited.

*The issue of voluntary as contrasted with public *auspices* for programs is separately discussed later.

Effects

It is traditional in "ideal" policy and programming discussions for the analysis to move directly from review of services rendered and of costs to an analysis of effects and differential effects. The questions are: what is offered? at what price? what is achieved? at what unit cost? and for whom? But, in the real world of social services, harsh realities intervene and generally defeat this logic.

The problem of effects has historical roots. Traditional nineteenth- and early twentieth-century voluntarism was its own justification; providing an outlet for individual good works, its religious merit was an overriding consideration. No one asked whether the recipient was actually helped, since it was assumed that what was offered as charity was received as such, and that good motives automatically assured effectiveness.

Furthermore, traditionally, many social services have had manifest or latent social control goals, and effectiveness could be seen or assumed: criminals and delinquents were locked up or supervised in the community; mentally ill people were removed to institutions; poor people were fed enough, so that they did not riot or die of starvation; abusive parents were warned or jailed; unwed mothers were made to see that they had acted improperly and were guided toward personal reform. Along similar lines, if settlement houses, Ys, boys' clubs, and other character-building services reflected the controlling ethic and stressed acculturation, skill training, or socialization congruent with the dominant ethic, few questions were raised about effectiveness.

To some extent, then, the matter of proven effects has and will probably continue to have low priority for many citizens, when raised with reference to social services. If activities and outlook are in harmony with cultural trends and the programs are provided by a voluntary or public service system that—in context—is defined as charitable or humane, large elements of the public will raise few questions. Volunteer tutors, "gray ladies," "big brothers" are manifestly good—and not to be questioned. Public community centers and pools, community lunches, foster homes, marriage counseling, are obviously needed and "worthwhile."

Yet, as controversy arises about social strategies, the matter of effects cannot be ignored simply on the grounds that the programs involved are compatible with other things on the social scene and have gained acceptability with many citizens. If there is a debate about income, political power, and social service strategies as alternative pathways out of poverty, should the evidence for each not be assessed? Similarly, if there are controversies within a social service field about the validity of different programs or the relative effectiveness of given techniques, should one forgo evidence? For example, can it not be determined whether a Head Start program improves a child's chances of succeeding in elementary school, and whether the existence of such a program brings about changes in the basic elementary school programs—both identifiable goals of the effort? Can we not find out whether probation, at a relatively low per capita cost, is or is not as effective as the more expensive residential treatment? whether counseling with all family members as a group is or is not more effective than work with individual members one at a time? Is it not possible to know whether group "encounter" approaches to changing addicts of various kinds via social psychological pressures of a peer group are more or less lasting than medical strategies?

For the policy planner and programmer there is no way to evade the responsibility of such questions, lest services merely gravitate from fad to fad. Yet hard data about effects are scarce in policy debates. Specific assertions are difficult for a number of reasons.

1. Social services are usually initiated at a time and in a place where *many other things are going on* (viz. the multiple innovations of the New Deal at a time of major political and value shifts in the society, or the services of the U.S. antipoverty war in the context of the civil rights movement and the Vietnam escalation). If the objective is large-scale effects, it is usually impossible to isolate the amount of change attributable to the specific social services innovation. William Gorham was reflecting a widely shared perspective when he reported, after a period of experimentation within the Department of Health, Education, and Welfare with a planning-programming-budgeting-system (PPBS):

Let me hasten to point out that we have not attempted any grandiose cost-benefit analyses designed to reveal whether the total benefits from an additional million dollars spent on health programs would be higher or lower than that from an additional million spent on education or welfare. If I was ever naive enough to think this sort of analysis possible, I no longer am.[11]

Major innovations in service will always be carried out in conjunction with other major innovations or significant political or social change. The society will often need to react to and evaluate such innovations without having solved the complex research problems of control, isolation of variables, and measurement.

2. *Value components cannot be avoided in evaluation,* and in a diverse country different population elements and regions emphasize their own value perspectives. Again, quoting Gorham:

The benefits of health, education, and welfare programs are diverse and often intangible. They affect different age groups and different regions of the population over different periods of time. No amount of analysis is going to tell us whether the Nation benefits more from sending a slum child to preschool, providing medical care for an old man or enabling a disabled housewife to resume her normal activities. The "grand decisions"—how much education, how much health, how much welfare, and which groups in the population shall benefit—are questions of value judgment and politics.[12]

Large social policy choices are made in value terms and political perspective, not through weighing of effectiveness. But even the measurement of effectiveness where it is seen as urgent and relevant does not escape controversial value choices: Is divorce "success" or "failure" as a family counseling outcome? Is placement of an old person in a nursing home "good" or "poor" service? What of the giving up of an out-of-wedlock child for adoption, the dropping out or continuance in school by an adolescent, the mastery of contraceptive technique by another unmarried adolescent, the organization of a protest group to combat or fight a public housing authority? Clearly, then, value components exist in the criteria that are posited by researchers and administrators in all measurement efforts and in evaluating the results obtained. Only those studies of effectiveness are possible which can resolve the difficult value choices inherent in defining success. Furthermore, only those studies will be taken into account whose criteria of effectiveness coincide with the basic expectations of those to whom the studies are addressed.

3. *Many social services or service components are not sufficiently standardized* to permit generalization from a given evaluation effort. Thus, well-publicized studies may show counseling ineffective with "potential" delinquents or casework unable to resolve problems of multiproblem families, but they are readily

dismissed by those who claim that service inputs were below standard in the given experiments.*

To illustrate from other social service fields: Failures of foster care may be attributed to poor screening of foster parents or successes to unusual and atypical care in selection. The outcome of a homemaker program may be ascribed to the typicality or atypicality of the specific personnel. Congress may complain that its investment in social services yielded no noticeable effects in rehabilitating AFDC families (1962 Social Security Act Amendments), while a research group may respond that no results were to be expected: there was insufficient availability or utilization of social services in public assistance in the one state studied intensively.[13]

In short, even where one would undertake modest studies of effects and effectiveness, as appropriate, there are complex research problems of control, outcome criteria, and standardized service ("inputs").[14] The interplay between these true obstacles, on the one hand, and the traditions that question whether one should probe too closely for effectiveness of services that reflect benign humanitarianism and charity, on the other, creates overwhelming blockages to evaluation. A situation results in which too little can be said with high degrees of certainty even where it would be reasonable to ask for evidence. However trite and repetitive the call, students of social services must urge that in any given field policy planners and programmers exploit research and evaluation reports to the fullest degree possible and that selective and expert evaluation be given high priority as new programs and agencies are developed and old ones renewed and reformed.[15]

It would appear reasonable, in a total social service strategy for a given territorial unit, to expect the following components in an "effectiveness package":

1. *Social indicators*—ongoing social statistics and indexes based

---

*This type of critique, readily sustained, decreased the usefulness of three expensive, extensive, and promising efforts to evaluate casework and personal counseling. Casework critics and planners will nonetheless continue to rely upon the results of these studies unless or until there appear equally careful and extensive efforts whose experimental services are deemed competent by professionals and that yield more impressive results. See Edwin Powers and Helen Witmer, *An Experiment In The Prevention of Delinquency* (New York: Columbia University Press, 1950); Henry Meyer, Edward F. Borgatta, and Wyatt C. Jones, *Girls at Vocational High* (New York: Russell Sage Foundation, 1965); and Gordon E. Brown, *The Multi-problem Dilemma* (Metuchen, N.J.: Scarecrow Press, 1968).

on them, compiled routinely and over time, to measure the state of social sector "health" and thus presumably reflecting the results of a diversity of measures. The conceptual and methodological problems are many, but interest in indicators has developed and significant work has been done since the early 1960s.[16]

2. *Carefully designed and controlled evaluation studies* to determine the specific effects of new, experimental, significant, controversial, or otherwise important programs. Such studies are costly and difficult. They should be carefully selected and then done well, and their results considered seriously.

3. *Cost-benefit studies* to select from among competing methods of known or discoverable effectiveness those which deliver the most service of acceptable consequence, at lowest per-unit cost.

4. *Channels for consumer response and evaluation* to provide holistic judgments about services. While user evaluations may not tell or scientifically measure exactly what is right or wrong, they tell something that is central to the enterprise: how those for whom a service is designed experience and evaluate it and how they would improve it.

Some progress is being made in all these categories and in relation to many social service fields.[17] Recently cost-effectiveness studies have been developed in many new fields and, where they ask modest questions and avoid efforts to quantify "human gains," they are useful. Movement toward client participation and community control has increased the sources of consumer feedback about programs, and follow-up and evaluation studies have been successfully pursued in some fields. The social indicators experiments are at a beginning phase, but promising.

For present purposes one must cite evidence of considerable service failure in many fields (state training school recidivism, foster home replacement, family agency case dropouts), of overlapping, wastage, and lack of service access. Many consumers indicate that agencies do not offer the help needed; many agencies proclaim clients to be "unmotivated" or unable to use help. There also is evidence that popular services exist on too small a scale to meet needs as users see them: the waiting lists for day care, homemakers, and public housing serve as illustration. Finally, there is evidence that agencies often become mired in their interventive repertoires and organizational structures to a point where the innovators must begin anew, often in unorthodox settings and without a community's formal backing. To illustrate, we note that most of the attractive, innovative, adolescent social services of 1970 seemed to develop outside of the traditional social agency family—as young people created self-help programs to cope with drug "emergencies" and related problems.

These impressionistic generalizations rely on reports and studies, but rest on too little empirical evidence to permit quantification. Equally impressionistic and imprecise are a group of positive findings: Certain services remain popular with their constituencies and usually face waiting lists. Some programs routinely achieve results that all observers are willing to evaluate positively. When disadvantaged people are given a voice in the expenditure of funds they often want to duplicate or expand traditional services.

As one adds the positives and the negatives, analyzes the uncertainties and the controversial, it is clear that there is reason for concern. Much is done with little evidence of success, much evidence of dissatisfaction, and considerable evidence of failure. There is no escaping the search for innovation, more knowledge, better-ordered service priorities. While there is no case for deserting the social service system in the interim, since some needs are being met or needs exist which people want to have met, there is also no substitute for efforts to develop measurement tools and methods that will facilitate more rational sorting out of the effective and ineffective—and some choices by specified criteria.

We shall note, in the subsequent discussion of policy approaches, that operations research and systems approaches often emphasize efficiency and outcome criteria as the major or sole basis for choice. Others posit different values as particularly relevant to the social services. While the latter have a strong case, since it is in the nature of social welfare to go beyond efficiency, there is no logic to closing our eyes to unit costs, effects, and effectiveness. The fact that lofty rhetoric is used to justify policy is no excuse for ignoring the questions of what actually occurs, what is achieved, and how consumers feel about it.

What of the considerable practice-oriented research into the social services? Does this not make a policy contribution?[18]

The answer depends on the intent of the question. Much research into the social services is actually basic social science research employing social service materials. As such it is not specifically oriented to helping policy makers or to answering questions about effects and effectiveness. Appropriately employed, it may nonetheless aid the analyst. Much of the research is oriented to what might be called practice issues: how to select foster parents, the grouping of children in institutions, the differential response to different interviewing or treatment techniques. As such it may contribute to the work of the individual practitioner and to administrative decisions on the immediate level. The relevance to larger issues depends not only upon design but also upon the ability of a policy analyst to relate it to other studies that, in their totality, may shed light on significant questions.[19] Some of the research is very relevant to questions of need and user response to service— this too may be applied by the analyst to policy questions. Finally, there has been only a limited amount of research focused specifically on policy questions, but interest has begun to develop and expansion is anticipated.[20] New organizational structures have been created to foster such development: policy centers and comprehensive programmatic research enterprises.

Needs?

In an interesting critique of a major British report on the social services, Peter Townsend emphasized the committee's failure to relate services to needs.[21] Our discussion of programs and personnel may be similarly faulted. More specifically, Townsend argued that while the formulation of goals may be influenced by opinions of consumers and suppliers of service, as well as by conventional views of need and standards of service, one should also attempt objective assessment of needs and standards: "Needs can be shown to exist independent of the feelings engendered within a particular society and independent of those recognized by society's institutions."[22] One would, in Townsend's strategy, seek several measures of inequality and of deprivation and relate these to objectively developed standards of service, as part of the social service planning process.

We have not attempted such analysis, since the present undertaking makes no pretense of social service planning for a field or locality. Our goal, rather, is to define the parameters of general social services in the United States and to provide sufficient illustrative detail to introduce current policy issues. Such issues would be of concern to planners and programmers on all levels.

Clearly, Townsend's logic is right for those who would plan

services at a given time and place. The complexities are enormous. To illustrate:

1. Basic physical requirements for clothing, shelter, and essential caloric intake aside, most "needs" are conditioned by societal context and the expectations engendered. Indeed, the form and level of need satisfaction is culturally set.

2. Service standards (number of teachers per 100 pupils, number of doctors per 100,000 population, and so on) are occasionally validated empirically as assuring a defined level of service. More often they incorporate some elements of folklore and faith. They always assume a specific pattern of operations, and the pattern may not be acceptable to innovators and reformers.

3. What is need satisfaction at one time and what is an acceptable service pattern at a given point become outmoded as aspirations change in response to greater affluence, improved communication, scientific progress, and so on. Indeed, policy decisions (about equity-equality, for example) affect levels of expectation.

Thus, while one might at a given time and place solve the "needs" problem in the sense of arriving at definitions and agreements that would empirically compare social deficits with resources assigned to cope with them,[23] it would not serve our purposes in the present volume to go beyond the illustrative and incomplete survey of some social services already presented.

Considerations such as these also make it undesirable here to attempt an assessment of the *resource* picture presented in the earlier expenditures section. As needs are redefined and standards reformulated, a program's service deficit may be computed. This, then, becomes one of a series of competing claims upon the country's productivity. The decision as to the size of the allocation is of course affected by the nature of the other claims that arise, the values that are dominant, and the distribution of power among competing claimants.

One may ask whether assignment of more resources to social services would change or redefine the policy issues of the next section. The answer is yes in the sense that fewer choices would have to be made if resources were plentiful; more diversity and acceptance of opposites might be tolerated (public-voluntary, integrated-separatist, cash-in kind benefits, and so on). The reality is that resources are always scarce and never unlimited. Furthermore, some of the policy alternatives *are* mutually exclusive, or at least do affect one another. Finally, availability of resources for a given field is also affected by policy choice since—in turn—it influences the creation of a constituency and the costs of implementation. We doubt, therefore, that most policy analysts can begin by efforts to define and solve the resource side of the equation.

For present purposes we have noted:

1. The relatively low current priority assigned what we call general social services within the totality of social welfare (social service) expenditures
2. Illustrative evidence that general social services may be considered quantitatively and qualitatively inadequate almost everywhere
3. An analysis of social change in modern society that suggests that social services will be essential in the predictable future and perhaps should be given a higher priority if certain amenities and protections are not to be ignored
4. The urgency of innovation and social invention, which would make any long-term quantitative projections out of present service patterns quite insufficient.

In sum, if the society is responsive to need and unless there is great constriction in productivity, social services are destined to continue—even to grow—and to change. Those who would guide this development cannot ignore issues of policy.

NOTES

1. Ida C. Merriam and Alfred M. Skolnik, *Social Welfare Expenditures Under Public Programs in the United States, 1929–66,* Research Report no. 25, Office of Research and Statistics, Social Security Administration (Washington D.C.: Government Printing Office, 1968). Annual analyses to supplement this report appear in the *Social Security Bulletin.*

   Our exclusion of education, health, and housing in the discussion of general social services, and the nature of available reporting systems, inevitably leaves out certain activities that many would list as social services in the narrower sense—but the omissions do not distort the basic relationships (social services to all social welfare) and are currently the only practical approach.
2. The S. M. Miller and R. Altschuler esitmates appear in unpublished early draft of projected Volume 2 of *Services for People* for the Task Force on Organization of Social Services, Department of Health, Education, and Welfare, 1968.

3. Good points of departure in seeing programs from the perspective, usually, of the responsible administrative agencies are the following: *Encyclopedia of Social Work, Sixteenth Issue,* 2 vols. (New York: National Association of Social Workers, 1971); *Statistical Abstract of the United States,* U.S. Department of Commerce, Bureau of the Census (Washington, D.C.: Government Printing Office, 1972); *Human Needs; Social Security Bulletin; Aging; Children Today;* U.S. Department of Health, Education, and Welfare. Reports from the National Center for Social Statistics and for the Public Health Service. Also see reports from the Family Service Association of America, Child Welfare League of America, and other national voluntary planning and coordination agencies cited in the text. For contrast, see *Social Trends* for 1971 or 1972, from the United Kingdoms' Central Statistical Office (Her Majesty's Stationery Office), or see the latest edition of *Social Welfare of the Northern Countries* (Stockholm: Annual).

4. "Children Served by Public Welfare Agencies and Voluntary Child Welfare Agencies and Institutions, March, 1970," Report E–9, National Center for Social Statistics, Department of Health, Education, and Welfare, March 1970.

5. For a guide to the complex series of programs, see "Child Care" in Charles L. Schultze, et al., *Setting National Priorities: The 1973 Budget* (Washington, D.C.: The Brookings Institution, 1972), pp. 252–290.

6. For example, see Hyman Weiner, et al., *The World of Work and Social Welfare Policy* (New York: Regional Research Institute in Social Welfare. Columbia University School of Social Work, 1971). Also, see United Nations, Department of Economic and Social Affairs, *Industrial Social Welfare.*

7. Sar A. Levitan, "Manpower Programs for a Healthier Economy" (Washington, D.C.: Center for Manpower Studies, George Washington University, 1972).

8. See Charles Grosser, *Community Organization: From Enabling to Advocacy* (New York: Praeger, 1972).

9. Roy Lubove, *The Professional Altruist* (Cambridge, Mass.: Harvard University Press, 1965).

10. See "Voluntary Action News," published regularly by the National Center for Voluntary Action, Washington, D.C.

11. William Gorham, "Notes of a Practitioner," in *The Public Interest,* No. 8 (Summer 1967). Quote from his testimony before the Joint Economic Committee, *The Planning-Programming-Budgeting System: Progress and Potentials,* 2 vols. (Washington, D.C.: Government Printing Office, 1967).

12. Ibid.

13. Handler and Hollingsworth, "The Administration of Social Service . . ."

14. Herbert H. Hyman, Charles R. Wright, and Terence K. Hopkins, *Applications of Methods of Evaluation* (Berkeley and Los Angeles: Univer-

sity of California Press, 1962); also, Edward Suchman, *Evaluative Research* (New York: Russell Sage Foundation, 1967).

15. For a useful review of the state of the art, see Henry Maas (ed.), *Research in the Social Services: A Five-Year Review* (New York: National Association of Social Workers, 1971. The manpower field has been subject to as much or more measurement and evaluation as any in the past decade. For an informed and wise appraisal of experience and assessment of possibilities see Sar A. Levitan and Robert Taggart III, *Social Experimentation and Manpower Policy: The Rhetoric and the Reality* (Baltimore: Johns Hopkins Press, 1971).

16. The topic is large and complex. How, when there is no conceptualization of "social system," which can be operationalized, does one develop indicators of the social health and characteristics of a society? How does one choose dimensions to monitor that have long-term normative significance? Given present sources and methods of collecting good statistics and current thinking about social factors, is there any way to aggregate statistics into major index items? For an introduction, see Raymond A. Bauer (ed.), *Social Indicators* (Cambridge, Mass.: MIT Press, 1966); Bertram M. Gross, *Social Intelligence for America's Future* (Boston: Allyn and Bacon, 1969); *Toward A Social Report,* U.S. Department of Health, Education, and Welfare (Washington, D.C.: Government Printing Office, 1969); Eleanor Bernert Sheldon and Wilbert E. Moore (eds.), *Indicators of Social Change* (New York: Russell Sage Foundation, 1969); and *Statistical Abstract of the United States, 1970,* U.S. Department of Commerce (Washington, D.C.: Government Printing Office, 1970). A sophisticated review of conceptual issues appears in Eleanor B. Sheldon and Howard E. Freeman, "Notes on Social Indicators: Promises and Potentials," *Policy Science,* 1, 1 (Spring 1970), 97–112. For a British illustration, see Muriel Missel (ed.), *Social Trends, No. 1,* Central Statistical Office (London: Her Majesty's Stationery Office, 1970). On the city level, an approach is offered in Martin V. Jones and Michael J. Flax, *The Quality of Life in Metropolitan Washington, D.C.: Some Statistical Benchmarks* (Washington, D.C.: The Urban Institute, 1971).

17. Maas, *Research in the Social Services* . . .

18. For example, see Henry S. Maas (ed.), *Five Fields of Social Service: Reviews of Research* (New York: National Association of Social Workers, 1966), and Maas (ed.), *Research in the Social Services. . . .*

19. As exemplified in the contribution of Kadushin in Maas, *Research in the Social Services* . . . in his summary of foster care and adoption research.

20. See Rothman and Carter in Maas, ibid. and p. 11.

21. Peter Townsend, "The Objectives of the New Local Social Service" in *The Fifth Social Service: A Critical Analysis of the Seebohn Proposals* (London: Fabian Society, 1970).

22. Ibid., p. 9.
23. For illustration of several approaches, see Eileen Younghusband, et al., *Living With Handicap* (London: National Bureau for Co-operation in Child Care, 1970); Jean Packman, *Child Care: Needs and Numbers* (London: Allen and Unwin, 1968); Florence Ruderman, *Child Care and Working Mothers* (New York: Child Welfare League of America, 1968); Alfred J. Kahn, et al., *Neighborhood Information Centers* (New York: Columbia University School of Social Work, 1966); Alvin Schorr, *Poor Kids* (New York: Basic Books, 1966); *Family Unit Register* (St. Paul, Minnesota: Greater St. Paul United Fund and Council, 1969).

Policy Issues

The Framework
of Social Service Policy

In deciding to develop or to expand social services, a group, organization, or government adopts a policy—as it does in electing one category of services rather than another for emphasis. Similarly, the designation of organizational forms for the services and the selection of a delivery system for any specific service represent significant policy choices. Such choices have consequences whether or not immediately visible during the choice process, and whether or not the choosing is deliberate, or even conscious.

What do we here mean by policy?[1] To the planner a policy is a "standing plan," a "guide to future decision making," or a "continuing line of decisions or set of constraints upon individual decisions." It is the implicit or explicit core of principle that underlies specific programs, legislation, priorities. "Social policy" may be described as the common denominator of decisions and constraints with reference to social welfare or social service programs. Or one may specify policy with reference to a given service system (family welfare, social insurance, and so on) or a given type of social issue (degree of localism, use of market-type instruments).

Policy questions raised about social services in the more distant past were quite different from the ones we are facing here. Before general social services began to serve people other than the poor and the unacceptably deviant (that is, before the late nineteenth century for the most part), there was little concern with the stigma associated with service. To those who rendered charity, for that is what the services were, there was no doubt that "it is better to give than to receive." To the general public it was acceptable or even desirable that charity be in some way constraining on the recipient or perhaps even punish him because of his need to accept aid. The notions of professional skill and specialization were generally not yet developed. If one wished to distinguish among the categories of people making use of services, it was so as to permit somewhat different moral assessments of various "clients." Thus, it might be held that children should not be kept with adults, dangerous criminals with the "impotent poor," or the extremely disturbed mentally ill with "innocent" women and children. Since the giving of help, the offer of aid, was its own justification and reward, there was little accountability for results from a user perspective (an arena in which change has been very slow). Therefore, questions of coordination, case integration, and service accountability did not often arise. And, given a view of the poor or the deviant that accentuated moral failure and inferiority, there was readiness to concentrate on "in kind" benefits and indoor (institutional) relief, approaches that appear to facilitate "control" of recipients, rather than upon cash, vouchers, and market-type devices.

What is the occasion today for the considerable attention to social service policy? Why do some—but by no means all—of the concerns reach the mass media, public debates, legislative bodies, and other political forums? The order of the listing of relevant factors varies with individual perspective.

First, more people from all social classes are affected by social services. The problems of the "invisible poor" may generate little interest and debate, but women of all classes care about day care. Citizens of many backgrounds are interested in treatment resources for drug addicts, in service for unwed mothers, in abortion counseling services, in facilities for senior citizens, and so on. Many citizens are concerned with communal solidarity and consider social services as a possbile vehicle for its achievement.

Second, the poor and disadvantaged have become quite visible. Certainly among the major factors in making the policy debate more general was the "rights" revolution. In the early and mid-1960s black leaders and their allies began to ask whether the scarcity of ghetto social services and the control of social services by public and voluntary groups outside of the ghetto community did not represent a kind of "welfare colonialism." In this connection they raised two kinds of questions. First, in the early 1960s they asked why ghetto residents had to go to central offices, why services were not in the neighborhoods of people to be served, why the controlling boards were always "downtown" white people. Later on they asked: Were the services appropriate? Were the priorities right? Did the existing balance among services not confuse the fundamental issues as ghetto citizens perceived them? In the latter connection, they increasingly cited the prevailing emphasis on therapeutic and adjustment services, when in their view the priority need was for education, jobs and job training, housing, and urban amenity.

From the mid- to late 1960s the critics of the system took another step. The antipoverty war had stressed work and work training, while playing down personal treatment. But, often graduates of training programs for the deprived could not find—or could not hold—jobs. The available jobs were frequently considered to be "dead ends." The local milieu did not change as much as people hoped through the community action programs that generated health, child care, and other social services, plus "participation." Now the charge was made that these were the wrong priorities. Some reformers turned their emphasis toward public welfare reform or the achievement of a minimum guaranteed income. Why not end poverty with money rather than with service? Others stressed "local power" as the target, seeing this as the dynamic for "basic" institutional change. General social service was either diversion or target, not a major instrument.

These were not the only factors that created awareness of the policy issues in social services. Both the commitment to end poverty and the increased alertness to economic growth and its relationship to an accelerated inflation have highlighted certain manpower issues. There is recognition of the increased proportion of the labor force available for both commercial and nonprofit services, of the reservoir of noncredentialed and unskilled manpower in search of work. The question arose, and became urgent in social policy, as to whether what had previously been defined as professional tasks in education, social work, and health could be restructured and subdivided to create nonprofessional roles. Initially the idea was attractive as a way of coping with manpower shortages, but by the late 1960s, as some professional shortages began to ease, the question arose as to whether the new trend was not in itself desirable: Were some jobs not made artificially inaccessible? Were the "noncredentialed" better qualified than degree holders or college graduates for certain jobs in the sense of knowing consumers and their needs, as well as localities and their resources?

Similarly, the need to assure responsiveness of services to ethnic and cultural diversity, particularly to the unique problem of urban ghettos, spurred a movement toward decentralization in social services by the mid-1960s (or, alternatively, the creation of locally based but centrally controlled service outlets). This trend, too, had wider ramifications. Society's response to increasing bureaucratization and the creation of large-scale organization has taken a number of forms. Recently, increased localization of outlets has become popular and indeed urgent. Even governmental authorities, long ready to increase centralization of power and resources in Washington, have sought to define a "new federalism," involving redistribution of funds ("revenue sharing") and power to lower levels. The policy debate about degree and modes of decentralization in social services is to be viewed in this context.

Concern with service effectiveness or cost effectiveness has also contributed to social policy alertness within social services. The search for increased domestic expenditure to deal with urban blight, poverty, and racial injustice has taken place in a time of fiscal stringency: war and war preparation have had first priority claim on the public fisc; inflation has been a major problem. Within government, increased adoption of cost effectiveness and program budgeting techniques, a trend that began with the defense establishment in the 1960s and spread to all federal departments, and to many state and local units as well, has tended to highlight issues of priority and policy.

While operations research, systems analysis, and other efficiency or "economizing" approaches were gradually applied in the period after World War II to plans for the development of natural resources and to defense policy and programs, they began to receive serious attention with reference to many aspects of the domestic scene during the Great Society. Economists and political scientists, in particular, responded to the increased emphasis on the domestic sector by adapting, or attempting to adapt, their policy-analytic approaches to new kinds of issues. This in turn has raised questions about traditional value perspectives in American social service policy and has introduced alternative options into the debate. It has also highlighted the need to reconcile the "efficiency" and the "other-value" orientations to social service policy, just as all American institutions, including the corporation, have begun to face the need to reconcile the "economizing" mode (rationality as profit optimization) with the "sociologizing" mode (an attempt to use a variety of values in judging the public interest).[2]

"Consumerism" has become a large and respected movement in American society. Ralph Nader's leads are being followed in many fields. Within the social services, concern with the indictment by the minority community, organized poor people, and youth has created a readiness to review effectiveness in relation to expenditure—as a phase of accountability. At the same time there are social service proponents who have cautioned against pragmatic and utilitarian approaches that would justify efficiency criteria while ignoring important societal processes, particularly the end of social solidarity—which is seen as a higher value.

For board members, administrators, budget authorities, and planners the proliferation of social services since the 1960s has generated yet another category of policy concern. By the mid-1960s a middle-sized or large American city had three overlapping systems of social services:

1. Those associated with *public welfare,* including mental hospital services (available to welfare recipients and the very poor and —in the case of child welfare—to some others)
2. Those serving the nonrecipients of public welfare, largely *working and lower-middle class* (voluntary family and child welfare, child guidance)
3. *Antipoverty programs* (for the ghetto poor but quite often separate from and hostile to public welfare)

The issue had become: given the proposals for new income maintenance programs separating the administration of cash assistance from nonmonetary social services, given the pressure to relate antipoverty programs to long-existing services, and given the evidence that fragmented services were costly, ineffective, and irresponsible—what should be done? This question led directly to many basic policy issues, particularly to the matter of universalism versus selectivity (see page 78) and to the public-voluntary pattern.

The most basic among all the factors encouraging attention to policy follows from all that has been said. It has become clear that, in seeking to solve its social problems and to achieve urban amenity, racial equality, communal integration, social justice, and an end to poverty, the United States will rely heavily upon social services as a prime instrument. Social mobility, greater individual opportunity, geographic mix, and distribution of specific goods can be implemented through social service programs. Furthermore, as suggested in our very first chapter, social services become increasingly important to all segments of society and all social classes in facilitating response to social change. Social services now are matters of great urgency to an urban-industrial society. But this projection does not answer questions of what and how; it does not resolve issues of social policy and programming strategy. Because the questions and issues are complex and have many political and economic ramifications, the social services debate arouses interest and feeling.

Social Services in an Institutional Context

Mention has already been made of the position that holds that social services are and have always been a means of diverting attention from the need for "more basic" institutional change. The allegation is true, we have noted, in the sense that unmet human need sometimes generates irresistible pressure for major social innovation and shifts in power relationships. Such shifts set off chains of circumstances with unpredictable outcomes. No one seriously contends, however, except perhaps the more diabolical among political revolutionaries or the naïve who assume that apocalypse leads inexorably to Utopia, that a serious case can be made for opposing all social services in the hope that significant changes will follow and that such changes inevitably will be benign. A more valid argument may occasionally be offered against specific services proposed, where it is shown that such services are likely, whether or not so intended, to defer or interfere with more basic or more favored measures: a self-help project where participation in an election contest is an alternative; services to develop personal insight where one might launch an economic program; services to care for children so that mothers may work, where what they may need is income so that they may remain home to care for their children if they wish to do so.

These illustrations suggest that the promotion of constructive institutional change may take the form of advocating and implementing social services—using the term broadly here to include education, health, and income maintenance. The pace and type of institutional change may be as much a matter of the *type* of social service created as of the presence or absence of any service at all. This is so because desired institutional change, as sought by reformers, must be understood as an evaluative category, describing a point on a continuum in which shifts in power relations, resource distribution, institutional procedures, overall policies, and program balance bring about qualitative, sought differences in distribution of resources, primary and secondary social relations, social structure, and culture. Social service policy and programming decisions may be important factors here, even though no one would argue that they represent the sole approach.

In this sense, then, for those concerned with general social services in the narrower sense of the present volume, the policy questions at a given moment may be formulated as follows:

1. Is this the time for investment of energy, attention, and resources in social services (as contrasted with economic or political measures), and if so what should be the "mix" among these several components?*
2. What "mix" is desirable of different types of social services—broadly conceived to include education, health, and housing, as well as the general social services?
3. What is the appropriate balance among cash, public social utilities (which we shall define as services available at user option

---

*Political and economic judgments are here called for—as well as data about program complementarities. The "art" is in primitive state. On the notion of "mix," as an alternative to the more traditional "priorities" approach, see Kahn, *Theory and Practice of Social Planning*, pp. 223, 229, 242, 243.

or status), and case services (services with a "diagnostic" doorway)?*
4. Among the general social services, particularly case services, what is to be the mix of concrete services (food, housing, skill training) and relationship services (counseling, casework, guidance, and so on)?

Social utilities and case services, two major concepts, are yet to be introduced. The expansion of public social utilities would indeed represent significant institutional change. These notions require some background discussion.

Social welfare history began with the assumption that most "normal" people managed satisfactorily on their own, through their own energies and resources and with the assistance of primary group members and such traditional institutions as work and church. Temporary catastrophe and personal misfortune (flood, drought, war, accident, depression) might require public intervention, but this was temporary. Social welfare was a "sometime" thing; it "withered away" if times were good. Of course, some people were incapable of managing on their own or they were morally defective and "exploited" others, expecting help when they should have been able to manage—these were the "unworthy" poor, the malingerers. Whatever programs proved necessary for them should have deterrent and control features and should avoid encouraging continued dependency.

This view of social welfare, now generally named the "residual" perspective, goes back to the seventeenth century, when the beginnings of organized provision in the modern sense were visible in the West. It expanded with industrialization. In the United States, at least, it had no serious challenge until the latter part of the nineteenth century and, again, during the Great Depression of the 1930s. It is a widely held view today, particularly where personal mobility is visible and elements of frontier tradition are strong.

A residual view of welfare tends to give almost sole emphasis to what may be called "case services" or what Willard Richan has named "social intervention." Case services are available by individual diagnosis or evaluation. They are intended to restore or enhance functioning in an individualized manner. The assumption is that an outside environmental force or a personal illness or

*A later section reviews the "cash" or "benefits-in-kind" debate.

problem is in the way of adequate functioning. Treatment or help will bring improvement or cure; the recipient is considered to be a patient.

But the residual view hardly describes the total social reality of an industrialized or a post-industrial society, and case services do not encompass all the necessary societal responses. It is now understood that a successful industrialized society generates new problems and new needs by virtue of its success. Technological advances in production, increasing worker productivity, may create unemployment because some workers are not required or because members of the existing labor force lack the required skills. Scientific and public health advances increase substantially the number of the aged who are alive for significant periods after retirement from the labor force, thereby generating new needs in the fields of health, housing, income security, leisure, protective services, and so on. This alternative or "institutional" view of social welfare holds that out of its normal functioning the society constantly develops pressure for new provision for meeting newly emerging needs. This is as legitimate and appropriate a process as was the process that created the basic institutions serving an agricultural or early industrial society—family, church, local government, guild, and so on. New institutions must be invented to meet new societal requirements, and the process should be understood and welcomed. Social welfare, if the term is employed to mean the societal provision or action to meet such needs, is thus a continuing and expanding aspect of the modern world.

The institutional view of social welfare gives support to the concept that some social services might be regarded as "public social utilities," rather than as case services. Even extreme laissez-faire-ists do not question the need for such communal services as a water supply, postal system, sewage system, public transportation, or highway network. These are the infrastructure of the industrial society, and their use does not bring any stigma. There may be user charges, and the system is constantly updated to reflect changed need as well. Similarly, some social services are generally accepted as representing social infrastructure, although the listing varies by place. Generally included are elementary and secondary schools, parks, libraries, museums, and some aspects of public health. Included in some places are general health services, junior or community colleges, family planning, housing, employment services, credit unions, and information and access services. Often proposed and sometimes provided are day care for young children, family or youth centers, and centers for the aging.

Where a system is widely accepted as a public social utility, it may take on its own institutional autonomy outside of the general social services field. This is true, as already noted, of education, medical care, public housing, and—to an extent—employment services.

Public social utilities may be divided into those available at user option (library, museum, general community center) and those available by user status (day care, center for the aged). The user is citizen, not patient.

The social planner and policy maker thus faces the issue, in contemplating new or improved social service, of clarifying the balance among case services (to be reached through diagnostic or evaluative channels) and public social utilities, including those available by user option and those open to individuals of defined statuses. A full social service system would apparently require a mix. Public attitudes and preference—and particularly the determination of whether user wish is to be regarded as the criterion of "need" for service—will determine the readiness to create a utility and will clarify whether the utility is to be completely "free" or, as in the instance of water or transportation, to be associated with some pattern of user charges.

Students of American social welfare will recognize that, just as modern cities currently suffer because of inadequate public physical utilities—note the new concern with transportation, water, antipollution devices, and housing—so do cities also suffer because of public social utility lags. There has been a poverty of social invention and a deficiency in public investment in the social sector. Cities now need to find new primary group supports, new facilities for the very young and for youth, new provision for the aged, new enrichments for family life. Some of the services will be "concrete"; others, "relationship." The topic should be at the heart of public policy in coming decades, and estimating whether a service is or is not to be organized as a utility will occupy planners increasingly.

Universalism and Selectivity

Closely related to the case service–public social utility dichotomy, and growing out of the distinction between residual and institutional approaches to social welfare, is the formulation that differentiates universal from selective approaches to social welfare.

Universalism is associated in Great Britain with the names of Beatrice and Sydney Webb and Sir William Beveridge. Particularly in the egalitarian atmosphere of World War II, it was decided to develop social welfare measures, especially social insurance, on a flat-grant basis. All would pay at the same rate and benefit at the same rate, a social minimum. All social services, envisaged as reflecting a social minimum conceived in social justice and nurturing equality of opportunity, were by their nature to be universal.

Universalism as an idea is appealing to people with democratic convictions. It breaks away from poor law notions that only the inadequate, the failures, need the resources of the social welfare system. Indeed, to the Webbs, it destroys poor law completely. Universalism also departs from the residual notion that social services are temporary and needed only in time of special stress or catastrophe. It encourages constant updating of social services in the light of social change. It recognizes the large part that social services play in the economy and manpower strategy of any society. It offers leverage to assure that social services are quality services: where services are for the poor or only for the "unworthy," one cares little for making them attractive. Where they may serve anyone, they must meet the standards expected of any general communal provision.

Why, then, would there be any doubt at all about a policy of universal social services? Why, in the late 1960s, when the issue was publicly debated in Great Britain and much of northern and western Europe, should there have been considerable public support of the alternative of "selectivity," a system whereby people become eligible for services only if they are below a specified income—that is, meet a "mean test"?*

Modern proponents of selectivity often agree that there should be some universal provision, some public social utilities, but they would limit this provision to a few high priority fields such as

---

*Ryan, in a recent volume, poses the distinction as between "universalistic" and "exceptionalistic" approaches. Given the considerable background of the issue and the available literature, there would appear to be no valid reason to introduce a new vocabulary. See William Ryan, *Blaming the Victim* (New York: Pantheon, 1971).

Steiner differentiates "subtle" from "crude" techniques in coping with poverty, with the former corresponding roughly with universalism, perhaps "tinged" by economic aggregate demand concepts. Gilbert Y. Steiner, *The State of Welfare* (Washington, D.C.: The Brookings Institution, 1971).

public elementary education, where the communal stake is obvious and high. They hold that universal provision in many fields sets a norm for a greater volume of use than a country can afford. It takes out of the market, and relieves individuals of the cost of, many items that they should seek out for themselves and pay for out of earnings. If they are poor or have no income, it is held, let people apply on a means-test basis for public aid. Then their service costs can be publicly met or free service provided.

After all, this position holds, any universal service must be paid for somehow. A service's universality could generate demand and encourage use where the individual would not accord it a priority were he to pay costs out of his own income. Where this occurs, services ranking low in consumer preference gain support through the tax mechanism.

There are, moreover, two very practical obstacles cited against universalism. First, whatever the views of public policy advocates, there are sizable elements in the population in significant numbers of places that do not conceive of some social services as generally needed. They regard such services as "all right" for people with special problems or needs, but simply do not believe that they should be designed and organized with the total population in mind. Second, services are expensive. Whatever the ideological stance, there are those who hold that universalism as a social service philosophy is simply unrealistic. Indeed, it was during the several recent European crises of public finance that a number of countries holding to strong democratic ideologies either added user charges or departed from universalistic approaches by introducing means tests.

It was yet another consideration that led to the strongest attack on universalism in theory and practice in the United States of the antipoverty war of the mid-1960s. A number of students of social policy and some local and national leaders felt that, if programs were universal, the very poor often failed to get their "fair share." It was held that the educated and informed, or those with some resources to employ, were guilty of "creaming" what was meant as general public provision. The more advantaged permitted services to reach "the poorest" only after skimming off the best of it. As evidence one could cite how the very poor did not get a fair share of the best public secondary schools and colleges; how publicly supported libraries, museums, and concerts were operated largely for the benefit of the middle class; how expensive tax-supported beaches could be reached only by private car owners; how the very poor mentally ill were incarcerated in state congregate-care facilities while the more advantaged received ambulatory care and outpatient clinical service—and so on.

The strategy in response to these problems inherent in universalism was, of course, the antipoverty war. A national agency, the Office of Economic Opportunity, was set up in the Executive Office of the President as advocate for, planner and implementer of services for, and instrument of "the poorest." Local counterpart agencies were funded and placed in the hands of boards more or less representative of, responsive to, or consisting of the most disadvantaged. Many new social services were designed on the premise of income-group separatism and provided with service delivery structures growing out of such policy. Unique staffing patterns followed. (It was several years before many voices were heard claiming that, once again, selectivity had been self-defeating: these special services for the poor were often stigmatizing and of poor quality.)

In short, the issue was joined. On the one hand, selectivity is a response to "creaming." Also (although the argument has a constituency that may not care about "creaming"), selectivity is an approach that protects the public purse and assures that limited resources go where they are most needed. In the economics vocabulary this latter point is summed up as "efficiency." Universalism, on the other hand, reflects egalitarian and social justice ideologies. It faces modern realities about the need for social services and is a response to the allegation that, because of considerable historical baggage, services designed for poor people tend to be poor services and to attract poor-quality staff. Selectivity by means tests creates stigma and limits the degree to which services are called upon by those who need them ("take-up").[3]

Searching for a resolution that might preserve a universalistic stance yet be realistic about resources, the British discussed in the late 1960s the employment of a "needs" test. One would not introduce the individual means test, but one might consider the special needs of geographic subunits (depressed areas) or of special deprived groups (the aged, minorities). Within a universalistic strategy there would be geographic or group preference. It has yet to be shown, however, that such an approach does not create stigmatized inferior service. The British have not renounced universalism. but the principle has suffered a degree of erosion by group selectivity and some imposition of income tests and user charges, as recent governments have sought to cope with economic problems.

Social service policy clearly will continue to deal with such matters. In the sense that an income tax form is a type of means test, it has been shown that stigma and status inferiority need not follow an effort to classify people by means. Affluent as well as poor parents in the United States quite readily submit income statements used routinely to determine the levels of college scholarships. The issue would, then, appear to be the generality and form of the means test, and how it is socially defined, not its existence. Conceptually, any diagnostic criterion is a needs test.*

The analysis would tend to confirm Mike Reddin's view[4] to the effect that one cannot choose universalism *or* selectivity as a sole principle. The issue is one of emphasis, context, and nature of a composite policy. A democratic and relatively industrialized society might debate a solution along the following lines: First, there might be implemented quite generally the distinction we have proposed between public social utilities and case services. Utilities by their nature are "universal." They would be employed at user initiative, since eligibility would be a matter of status (age, handicap, and so on) or one's wish or option. Case services would become available through intermediaries, expert "doorkeepers," who assess personal need. In neither instance would income affect access.

There would remain much room for maneuver in determining which utilities are to be paid for out of general revenue (that is, preferably progressive income taxes) and which are more efficiently used and appropriately funded by user charges. The community's stake in assuring access should certainly be the major determinant: Are users who cannot or will not pay to be encour-

---

*In "On the Stigma Effect and the Demand for Welfare Programs: A Theoretical Note," an unpublished "discussion paper" from the Institute for Research on Poverty, University of Wisconsin (1971), Burton A. Weisbrod suggests, from an economics perspective, that it may be useful to think of "marginal stigma cost." The importance of stigma depends upon benefit levels, he believes: "with an increase in benefits it pays to incur greater stigma costs." The matter requires research. For some findings that ran contrary to expectations about AFDC, see Joel F. Handler and Ellen Jane Hollingsworth, The "Deserving Poor": A Study of Welfare Administration (Chicago: Markham Publishing Co., 1971).

aged? Would fees close the doors to those the community wishes to attract? Is the priority high enough to merit public funds?

Since case services always reflect personal or familial need and signify presence of a problem in adjustment or functioning, readiness to pay charges should never be an access factor. Nor should mode of payment determine the quality of service. Universal insurance—with public payment of premiums for the poor—or general revenue funding would appear desirable for case services. User charges are defensible only for increments, enrichments of services (private hospital rooms, a particular summer camp), reflecting personal preference rather than communal stake, or where they are clearly not factors in access to and employment of the needed case service.

Societies that accept such an approach to the universalism-selectivity issue will need to adapt it in light of the degree of their wealth, service development and manpower resources. Less-developed societies will have little choice but to begin with more selectivity in the earlier stages of the development, employing individual means tests or giving priority to specified groups.[5] Day care for favored factory workers or workmen's compensation for the labor force in a pioneer industry illustrate this approach. All societies may assign special priorities to underprivileged groups or regions.

A final comment: Completeness would suggest a third category, so that the policy options referred to here would be labeled as "universalism," "selectivity," and "exceptionalism."* Studying programs of aid for poor veterans, Steiner has shown how "superior" or "special" programs are developed in response to strong political pressure by veterans' lobbies, even though there is no rational justification for such positive discrimination or preference ("separate and unequal"). A special rhetoric and administrative machinery is invented for veteran relief to avoid stigma. Veterans receive aid for nonservice-connected disabilities and face rules about assets, earnings, dependents, and so on, quite different from those which apply to nonveterans.

Exceptionalism is a policy that could be defended if it paved the way for others, as did the successive separation of several disadvantaged categories from the "poor law" mass in the nineteenth

---

*Here exceptionalism means a favored category, unlike Ryan's sense of the term, which makes it synonymous with "selectivity." See footnote on page 79.

and early twentieth centuries. The Steiner studies appear to demonstrate that, in the case of veterans, the possibility of exceptionalism allows society to ignore the plight of others served by inadequate programs.[6]

Social Service "Rights" and the "New Property"

Students of social policy have in recent years talked increasingly of "the new income" and "the new property," seeking to call attention to the fact that one's standard of living depends in the modern world not only upon monetary income but also upon access to guaranteed assets, services, and resources.[7] Particularly relevant to social policy are pension and social insurance entitlements, housing, and broadly conceived social services such as education, health, and neighborhood amenities for recreation and leisure. Charles Reich and Harry Jones have elaborated a legal doctrine that argues, in effect, that this "new property" is as critical as is one's wage income and that the enactment of income security and social service legislation represents the conferring of property rights that can subsequently be protected in the courts.

It will be recognized, immediately, that such doctrine would tend to develop and flourish in the atmosphere of universalist social policy. While even Elizabethan poor law placed certain obligations upon the local parish for relief of some categories of the needy, thereby by implication assuring the latter of certain benefits, perhaps as a matter of right, the essential attitude to pre-poor law and poor law social provision is that it represented charity and individual beneficence, not the meeting of statutory obligation. In the United States, for example, President Pierce in 1854 vetoed a congressional grant of considerable acreage in support of mental hospitals on the grounds that the Constitution did not permit the federal government to enter into welfare activities. It was argued routinely that no precedent should be set that would seem to imply that welfare services or financial assistance may be regarded as a commitment of government and a right of recipients.

The changes in philosophy occurred initially in services that were to be universal. Elementary education was first privilege, then right, then requirement; a rights conception was essential if attendance for the young was to be made compulsory, an inevitable development in a society demanding literacy for labor force and political reasons. A variety of types of social insurance were enacted, beginning with the twentieth century, mandating in very specific terms participation in financing by employers, employees, and government and specifying the risks covered and the conditions for the award of benefits. The social insurance provisions of the 1935 Social Security Act were quite specific in this regard: payroll deductions and employer taxes were precisely defined, as was the pattern of benefits. Thus, government could enforce the law as it related either to responsibilities for insuring oneself or one's employees, or to the setting up of state employment services. Authorities could demand precise implementation of the law as it specified the exact financial benefits for a person of a given salary level; years of work; age of retirement, disability, or death; and number of dependents. A true legal right, in the social insurance sense, is a justiciable right; if benefits are not paid under the specified conditions and in the specified amounts, the claimant may call upon the power of the courts. Such right is the reciprocal of concomitantly specified obligations.

The concept is confused because the word "right" is also employed in the moral sense, as in the U.N.'s International Declaration of the Rights of Children or in similar affirmations made by many bodies over the years in many fields. It is further confused because some so-called rights are actually partial, justiciable in only a limited sense. As interpreted by the courts for many years, for example, public assistance in the United States was such a partial right. An applicant could demand court action if he could show that policies and grant levels were not uniform as among jurisdictions within a state or as among groups. However, he could do nothing in the courts if the state legislature had appropriated so little money that welfare departments could meet only a portion of need as computed under their own budget standards.

Similarly, if a state or city developed a public housing program, there might be limited legal recourse in instances of discrimination, personal abuse, or the imposition of restrictions on tenants that infringed on fundamental constitutional rights. However, there was no justiciable "right" to housing, no matter how frequent the moral affirmations in this realm (usually in the preambles of housing acts), that could compel public authority to offer adequate provision and on a scale to meet all need. Nor is there as yet—despite progress. A dynamic does seem operative, converting some "moral" rights to partial and then complete legal rights. Yet the total amount of achievement with regard to social services remains limited.

For the fact is that a true rights concept has reached social services only gradually and in a modest sense, elementary and secondary education in most places in the United States, community college and four-year college in a few; limited medical and hospital service, on an insurance basis for some and means-test basis for others; social insurance; a scattering of other areas, with little uniformity throughout the country; some aspects of veteran programs.

The latter part of the 1960s saw the development of neighborhood legal services as part of the antipoverty program; and a series of court challenges in "class actions" of administrative practice in public assistance and housing began to increase the rights component in a sense that certain administrative rules were defined as infringing on constitutional rights—residence laws, "man in the house" rules, unannounced home visits. At the same time Congress specified the one-time raising of grant levels to reflect changes in the cost of living, without mandating minimum levels as the point of departure. The President in 1969 urged Congress to enact a federal assistance minimum, but the Congress adjourned, stalemated on the matter. Even less progress has been made in housing, but here, too, one could illustrate an increase in the rights component.

In such an atmosphere, it was also inevitable that some attention would be directed to the right to more general social services such as day care, family counseling, child welfare, services for the mentally retarded, family planning, institutional care, rehabilitation, and so on. In a few instances higher courts sustained the claim that a child had to be returned to his home if an institution to which he had been committed as a delinquent could be shown as unable to provide the help he was deemed by the committing judge to need. In at least one state a mental hospital patient was awarded substantial damages because inadequate treatment was considered the cause of long confinement and consequent loss of earnings.[8] A court instructed one state exactly how institutional care for the mentally retarded was to be improved (Alabama, 1972). The concept has increasingly been advanced that if the state takes corrective or protective action, if it mandates placement or confinement, it simultaneously assumes the obligation to provide adequate services and thus establishes rights for those taken into care. Less definitively, in some cases of handicap judges have mandated that agencies offer certain specified help, thus creating a "right." In most other instances, general social services of a voluntary type have remained a privilege, not a right, no matter how urgent the services might be deemed in a "new property" sense. In fact, even protective-corrective programs seldom display a rights preoccupation.

In an early deviation from this trend in the mid-1960s, the Advisory Council on Public Welfare recommended to the Secretary of Health, Education, and Welfare that steps be taken to develop within the public welfare system comprehensive social services "readily accessible as a matter of right at all times to all who need them."[9] While, with reference both to income assistance and to social services, the report refers to application process, appeals machinery, legal aid, and publication of rights, it does not confront the issue (with reference to nonmonetary services) of how a service level and range can be statutorily specified, protected, and financed. Nor is it clear how courts are to become sufficiently expert and to achieve the staffing essential to mandating and overseeing service rights as they did school desegregation in the South.

As the "new income" and "new property" philosophies of the welfare state develop (and this would appear almost inevitable in a highly urbanized industrial society), the rights question cannot be long avoided. More serious attention may be expected to the question of the right to social service and exactly what this may mean. At the very least, if a service is defined as a right it must in some sense be standardized.

To the extent that such services are seen as universal public social utilities, whether available by user option or by user status, the answer would appear to be clear: If a service is meant for all citizens or for all children or all old people, infringments on access are interferences with statutory rights and may be dealt with as such by the courts. This does not, however, eliminate the problem of assuring legislative and administrative action to assure sufficiency of services quantitatively and their qualitative adequacy. Do social services lend themselves to sufficient specification for such purpose? Elementary and secondary education offer an encouraging precedent, but many social services are far less specified. Moreover, in many of the areas of concern, the mere provision of service will not of itself completely accomplish the objective. It

88   **Policy Issues**

will require considerable development of doctrine and provision
to assure actual access to services on the part of those eligible
and in need before the right may be said to be in existence.

With reference to case services, the rights notion may perhaps
translate itself into adequate machinery for case finding, evaluation, referral, case integration, accountability, and assurance that
a case so located and processed will not be dropped except in
relation to well-defined community policy and by the actions of
clearly designated community instruments. The approach to con-
tagious disease in medicine may offer a precedent, perhaps, in
relation to abused children, adjudicated delinquents and criminals,
and victims of certain addictions. The analogy becomes more
uncertain as one enters the field of those case services which do
not cope with situations of "clear and present danger" to self or to
community. The entire doctrine of rights as it applies to general
social services thus remains in an underdeveloped state and subject to further exploration, experiment, and analysis.

NOTES

1. See Alfred J. Kahn, *Theory and Practice of Social Planning* (New York:
   Russell Sage Foundation, 1969), Chapters 5, 6, 7, and *Studies in Social
   Policy and Planning* (New York: Russell Sage Foundation, 1969); Martin
   Rein, *Social Policy: Issues of Choice and Change* (New York: Random
   House, 1970), esp. Part 2; and Richard Titmuss, *Commitment to Wel-
   fare* (New York: Pantheon, 1968), Chapter 1.
2. On the latter distinction, see Daniel Bell, "The Corporation and Society
   in the 1970's," *The Public Interest,* No. 24 (Summer 1971). For a review
   of the various policy approaches in the "optimization" tradition, see
   Richard Zeckhauser and Elmer Shaefer, "Public Policy and Normative
   Economic Theory," in Raymond A. Bauer and Kenneth J. Gergen (eds.),
   The Study of Policy Formation (New York: Free Press, 1968), pp. 27–
   102.
3. For a recent American case for universalism, defined as "services good
   enough for any American," see *Services for People,* Report of the Task
   Force on Social Services (Washington, D.C.: Department of Health,
   Education, and Welfare, 1968), pp. 37–38. The British discussion is
   reflected in Mike Reddin, "Universality Versus Selectivity," in William
   A. Robson and Bernard Crick (eds.), *The Future of the Social Services*
   (Baltimore: Penguin, 1970).
4. Reddin, "Universality Versus Selectivity."
5. For illustrative purposes The French perspective is presented by Pierre
   Laroque in "Human Rights, Social Work and Social Policy," *Interna-*

tional Social Work, 12, 3 (1969), 3–13. A British analysis is offered in Richard M. Titmuss, "Choice and 'the Welfare State'" and "Universal and Selective Social Services" in his *Commitment to Welfare* (New York: Pantheon, 1968), pp. 113–123, 138–152.

6. Steiner, *The State of Welfare,* Chapter 7.

7. In this connection, see S. M. Miller and Frank Reissman, *Social Class and Social Policy* (New York: Basic Books, 1968); Charles Reich, "The New Property," *Yale Law Journal,* 73, 5 (April 1964), 773–787; and Harry Jones, "The Rule of Law and the Welfare State," *Columbia Law Review,* 58, 2 (February 1958).

8. William J. Curran, "The Right to Psychiatric Treatment," *American Journal of Public Health,* 58, 11 (November 1968), 2156–2157.

9. *"Having the Power, We Have the Duty . . . ,"* Advisory Council on Public Welfare (Washington, D.C.: Government Printing Office, 1966).

4

Goals
Meet Technique

Redistribution as a Social Service Objective

One of the major tensions in social welfare policy arises from the differences in viewpoint between (a) those who assume that the purpose of programs is to aid the unfortunate and handicapped in the context of the economic and social status quo and (b) those who conceive of social welfare programs as an instrument of equalization. Indeed, it is the perception of this issue and the recognition that extensive social welfare programs may very well have some redistributional effects that lead some people to oppose the "welfare state" as socialist. On the other side, it is the potential for redistribution through both cash and "in kind" programs that leads other people to conceive of redistribution as the central justification for, and beacon light of, social policy.

What, then, are the facts? Serious study of the subject is only

recent, and there are many uncertain areas; yet several generalizations seem to be sustained. If by redistribution we mean a system of transfers of money and nonmonetary benefits so arranged
that members of a given group end with a balance different from
that which is created by market transactions, then we may
hypothesize:

1. Governmental taxation, grants and service programs, and various government-sanctioned and aided insurance and fringe-benefit
schemes are sometimes redistributional, but by no means always
in favor of the very poor or even of the working class.

2. Means-tested income maintenance programs are the most
clearly redistributional in favor of the severely disadvantaged;
other types of income maintenance may be less so or not at all.

3. Some social service programs, whether in the narrow or in a
looser sense of the term, are redistributional in favor of the most
disadvantaged, some in favor of other population elements.

These, at least, appear to be reasonable hypotheses for the
United States and Great Britain. The available research is limited,
and the need for further exploration of these matters has been
recognized by the United Nations.[1]

The nature of existing payment and service arrangements makes
these hypotheses almost inevitable. Income taxes are graduated,
but there are many loopholes available to the more prosperous
and to people in upper-income brackets. Because the sales tax
and social security tax are regressive and proportionately important to low-income people, their total tax "bite," as of this writing,
is of the same dimension (proportion of pretax income) as that of
upper-income people although some remedies are pending. The
U.S. Congress was unwilling until 1970 to eliminate income
taxes of $2 billion on those below a governmental poverty line.
Benefits to agriculture and corporate industry benefit the more
affluent, and the pattern of mortgage insurance and tax deductions
for mortgage interest and for real estate taxes may bias the governmental housing subsidy in favor of purchases of detached suburban dwellings. Income maintenance programs that use the
means test, largely public assistance, are redistributive but at a
low level. Social security income testing for the aged is very
limited, but there is some transfer from middle and high to low
wage earners in the pattern of benefits. Distinctions between capi-
tal gains and income aid the wealthy. Minimum wage laws are
positively redistributive for the poor but tend to lag behind infla-
tionary pressures.

Education, health, and housing—social services in the broadest sense—seem to be redistributive in favor of the very poor only as they emphasize a basic minimum (elementary school, which is compulsory, universal health checkup and inoculations). To the extent that they offer higher levels of education, more sophisticated or intensive health services, or housing that goes beyond the minimum, such programs may actually favor the more stable elements of the working class, the lower-middle class and even the upper-middle class. The sophisticated and informed, the people who know how to take advantage of possibilities, families motivated to get more for their children, do seek out and employ services that go beyond the compulsory minimum. Families with resources more often know about and have access to more programs. To illustrate, in some places secondary education and junior college, publicly paid, is of help only to the middle class because others cannot afford to have their children out of the labor market or cannot meet their daily expenses; in some places the best general hospital and outpatient psychiatric resources are employed by those who are knowledgeable, not by the most needy. The picture is blurred, however, varying among countries (some countries give all college students maintenance grants or salaries) and regionally in the United States.

To turn to general social services, the field of special inquiry in this volume, data about redistributional effects are very scarce, but there is a significant body of research about limited service utilization by the most disadvantaged, their high dropout and failure rates, and their general lack of access to the more sophisticated services.[2] In general, a program that is sharply selective, focused on a deprived group or depressed area, or available on a means-test basis, will have considerable redistributional impact (Head Start, public housing). It will transfer resources, in the form of services, from "haves" to "have nots."* A universal program, whatever its other merits, may or may not be redistributional, depending on its attractiveness to the poorer members of the community ("take-up") and on the system of information and access that affects the actual pattern of utilization.

It is this knowledge, as suggested in the discussion of "creaming" under the heading of "universalism and selectivity," which

---

*But if it spends a large proportion of its funds as salaries to "non-poor 'professionals'" or sales to middlemen (shopkeepers who handle food stamps), the effect is tempered.

led advocates of redistribution to favor such selectivist programs as the U.S. antipoverty program and to urge more jobs in social service programs for local, "uncredentialed," poor people. Proponents of these measures were prepared to risk the disadvantages of stigma and the allegation that programs for the poor are poor programs, in order to assure access by the underprivileged and a greater likelihood of redistributional effect.

Those who would argue for universalism in social service and who accept the redistributional goal must, in turn, consider ways in which guarantees of access by the most underprivileged may be built into such programs for redistributional effect. Just as redistribution, if that is a goal, may be achieved by passing new tax-wage-subsidy legislation, by enacting new policies, and by launching new programs, "one also achieves redistribution . . . by arrangements to facilitate access to the established rights, benefits, services, entitlements and to assure the actual delivery and use of intended services."[3] This makes relevant the entire subject of organization for service delivery at the local level (see page 149). It makes immediately salient such matters as (a) advice and information services, usually on a neighborhood basis; (b) case advocacy services; (c) complaint machinery; and (d) legal services.[4]

The specific techniques available to assure access, and the supporting developments in service organization and staffing, are discussed subsequently. Here we note only that the proposals are logically convincing but are not backed by hard research data on a significant scale. Evaluative studies are awaited.

At this point we must recognize, again, that the implied premise of the entire discussion, the desirability of utilizing social service programming for its potential redistributional effect, is also subject to the broad differences of opinion that prevail about all social policy, differences that have already been pointed to as going well beyond social service policy. The objections come from two wings of political opinion. There are those who would offer social services to assure equality of opportunity, not of condition (status). To them social service per se need be only modestly redistributional. Their purpose is to facilitate personal mobility by providing a foundation of capacity and skill. Others, who would utilize social services rather than jobs and market mechanisms to decrease inequality and to guarantee adequate levels of living, would go further in evaluating social services in their redistributional effects.

Inevitably, then, this more fundamental issue of social policy must be resolved before social service policies are fully confronted.*

Consumption vs. Investment

During 1972 the White House proposed several pieces of legislation to Congress, and the Department of Health, Education, and Welfare initiated a variety of administrative measures that emphasized a utilitarian concept of social services. Programs would be financed and developed to "overcome barriers" to economic self-maintenance among the unskilled, handicapped, or unmotivated. Measures would be promoted if they gave promise of removing people from institutions or increasing their capacity for self-care while living in the community. Program evaluation would focus upon "barriers overcome," in a progression from institutional care to community care of an intensive kind, to self-care to partial self-support, to self-support.

These proposals were attractive to many people who consider social goals diffuse and social service programs to be of questionable value. They were regarded as too constricted by critics who would also emphasize the developmental, socialization, and enrichment missions of the social services. In a modern form of the "residual" versus "institutional" debate in social welfare, these two opposing views represent what might be considered "consumption" versus "investment" positions.

American planners or programmers of social services seldom talk in terms of the investment-consumption policy issues, yet the concepts appear frequently in the international literature on development planning.[5] The policy maker will find them tricky, but not to be ignored.

In a sense, the tradition of social services in relation to private charity's benevolence or the humanitarian's social minimum would seem to support the notion that the service is a good unto itself; it provides funds or supplies for needed consumption by the disadvantaged or offers useful personal help. Yet brief exploration

---

*Theodore J. Lowi has formulated the relevant social policy options as distribution, redistribution and regulation. See his "American Business, Public Policy, Case-Studies, and Political Theory," *World Politics*, 16, 4 (July 1964), 677–715.

shows that, in fact, this has never quite been accepted as the sole mission of general social services. Something more has been sought. Elizabethan poor law demanded a work return from the able-bodied adult and child whether he was given outdoor aid or assisted in an institution. Private charity, at least that segment of it in the nineteenth century that evolved into family service agencies and child welfare programs (perhaps, in a sense, some settlements, too), clearly differentiated the "worthy" from the "unworthy" poor. The former clearly were seen as morally virtuous—or at least as salvageable; the assistance or combination of assistance and concern was clearly an "investment" in their rehabilitation. Their failure to follow the rules, to take advice, to reform was a cause for redefining them as unworthy of the aid of voluntary social agencies. They would be left for the more punitive and controlling poor laws authorities.

Child welfare literature, for example, quotes Charles Loring Brace, a pioneer, to the effect that a childless farm couple taking in young, homeless children would be assuring themselves at a future time both of a loving responsiveness and help on the farm. Earlier indenture arrangements ignored sentiments entirely: one "invested" in training an apprentice.

Settlement houses were focused on environmental ills as much as on individual adjustment problems. However, to the extent that they offered citizenship courses, woodworking training, dental clinics, child care, cultural activities, and boys' clubs, they often went beyond a desire to enrich peoples' daily experiences (consumption). Indeed, many of the pioneering settlement leaders spoke of the services as facilitating more rapid Americanization, promoting community adjustment and harmony, encouraging self-support, and decreasing deviance (investment).

In the world of Keynesian economics, another line of analysis appeared. Social service and income maintenance expenditures, if related to the state of the economy, could be an important instrument of demand management. A government would want some authority for "elastic" consumption. In recent years it has become clear, however, that expansion to spur demand is easy, but contraction to counteract inflation is politically difficult.

In short, social services have a tradition of both consumption and investment motivations. The rhetoric has favored consumption, while the latent, or unexpressed, motives were perhaps most often investment. There have been few who have supported non-instrumental social services.

Two developments have brought the policy issue—consumption or investment?—to the fore in recent years: the experience in organizing social services for developing countries and the anti-poverty program in the United States. The poor country that is seeking to industrialize and modernize finds itself facing very difficult choices. Should it rapidly make available to all the health protections and services that are technologically possible, because people have a right to them, and ignore the consequences (lower infant mortality in a country with major food shortages, for example, thus shifting the age and cause of death!). Or should this "consumption" approach be discouraged in favor of a strategy that says, "Let us target and time the new health services in relation to educational, feeding, and housing programs tied to the economic plan for an area?" This latter "investment" approach, which receives its rationale from the need to allocate scarce resources, forgoes humanitarian impulse for allocative efficiency.

Similarly, should universal elementary education be offered at once, to all children, because literacy is desirable and democratic, thereby commanding all resources that might be assigned to intermediate technical education and advanced training, or is an investment strategy to be developed for education? In the latter approach, resources are rationed among educational ventures on the several levels in accord with personnel demands posed by economic development—and to assure a gradual increase in the reservoir of teachers for the eventual universal system.

From these illustrations it becomes clear that at a given instant it may be difficult to determine whether the program is actually conceived in investment terms, or only so presented. In a sense, "consumption" and "investment" may become evaluative categories or public relations instruments that are politically employed in some contexts. Shifts in the definition of goals have political effect. Many of the proponents of stronger social service programs began in the 1950s and 1960s to talk of "investment in human resources," and they advocated social service programs as good development strategy.

To the social service planner the entire issue poses a serious dilemma. Conceptually, social services are goods and services made available on the basis of other than market criteria to facilitate socialization and individual development and to cope with problems. Why should one, therefore, distinguish some services as better "investments?" If a decision as to whether the offering of access to service is a good investment for society (a "market" question) must be introduced into the equation, this would appear to be contrary to the very function of social services. On the other hand, the planner knows that resources are always in short supply.

Much of the debate is confused by semantic difficulties as economists meet politicians and both deal with social welfare advocates. As Myrdal notes,[6] much talk about education and health as "investment" is naïve and uninformed, especially in developing countries where the effects of expenditure vary with whatever else is done about the institutional context in which expenditures are made. Politicians sense this, but also fluctuate between a rhetorical and precise employment of the investment term. Social welfare personnel, for their part, too often tend to ignore the fact that any given society must weigh its priorities and has a right to an "instrumental" view of social services. In this sense, however, criteria of desirability need not be derived solely from the marketplace. Societies attend to more than economic growth, productivity, and other such objectives if they would be just, humane, or politically viable.

A social service policy maker may find his way with such a posture. He may at a given time favor setting up a program and giving it priority because it meets urgent societal objectives ("opening opportunity" to minority groups), reflects the resource picture, and promises large payoffs ("investment" criterion); however, he may still consider the notion that of all the eligible individuals or groups, allocative priorities within the program should be assigned in accord with means, needs, and social justice concepts ("consumption" criterion). This is not to deny the constant pressure he will face to give service priority to those best able to fit into the program, since payoff will then be highest (again, "creaming"). But in social welfare, optimum output should not supercede need for and ability to *use* a service ("diagnostic" criterion).

In short, since money, materials, and skilled manpower remain in short supply, it is legitimate to introduce the "investment" issue among other criteria for choice. Few societies can afford large amounts of consumption that are not in some sense instrumental, or say that any consumption is good since it leads to economic growth. Developed and underdeveloped countries are inevitably focused on urbanization, industrialization, modernization, or specified problem solving. On the other hand, the notion of "investment" need not be tied only to narrowly conceived productivity payoffs.

Developments in the United States in the 1960s may be viewed in these terms. Several of the youth-opportunity mobilizations of the early 1960s, precursors of the antipoverty program, turned away from the more traditional approaches to delinquent young people. They decided not to expand personal counseling, group therapy, residential treatment, or Big Brother efforts. Instead, they would concentrate on education, job guidance and placement, and training—and on those aspects of role training that would prepare young people for the job market. The rationale was clear: working on the premise that many young men became delinquent because of lack of access to legitimate or to illegitimate means of success in the world of work and money (they had neither jobs *nor* rackets as sources of income and social status), these mobilizations concluded that the primary mission was to open opportunity. In fact, they often called their social services "opportunity programs." These were visibly intended as a social investment in offering legitimate channels for the activities of young people who might otherwise choose the illegitimate or would "cop out." Program success was to be gauged, not by the insight, happiness, or "adjustment" of the participant—or by whether similar investment in *others* would have better payoff—but by the participant's attainment of skill and his employment of that skill in the world of work.

This type of thinking, translated into the subsequent antipoverty war, tended to make the policy choice as between investment and consumption strategies more visible and more legitimate in a non-market-oriented social welfare. Indeed, the antipoverty war represented clear preference for "investment-type" programs: skill upgrading, small business development, agricultural loans, job preparation and placement, child development, and education. Cultural, character development, therapeutic, personal enhancement, and recreational "offerings" were given low priority, if acknowledged at all. It is therefore hardly a surprising matter to observe that the arrival of such an approach coincided with the introduction of "efficiency" approaches to planning and policy making in the public social welfare sector (see page 125).

The issue was presented dramatically late in 1969 in the differ-

ences between the day-care provisions of President Nixon's proposed Family Assistance Plan and the opposing approach of the
President's (Lyndon Baines Johnson) Commission on Income
Maintenance Programs (the Heineman Commission). President
Nixon argued that his new approach to income maintenance was
"workfare," not "welfare." To permit (indeed to *require*) mothers
of school-age children to enter upon training or work, the federal
government would subsidize creation of 450,000 new day-care
spaces by meeting 90 percent of costs of operation and facility
renovation. To which the Heineman Commission (reporting after
the Nixon proposals) responded that at a 1968 per capita cost of
$1,700 for Head Start service and given the earning power of the
typical AFDC mother, one could not conceivably regard this as a
good investment. If one wished to consider day care in child
development terms ("consumption"), other criteria would enter.

At this point several dissenting commission members argued
for day care in terms of increasing a mother's freedom of choice
about working and to assure more satisfactory care for children
who are at present cared for under dangerous and unhealthy conditions. (They also questioned the assumed per capita cost.) The
dissenters asked whether potential earnings of mothers are the
only criterion of return on a social investment like day care, citing
the program's preventive potential in relation to various kinds of
problems. In short, arguing in both investment and consumption
terms, another kind of case for expanded day care was made.[7]

This exploration tends to suggest that the policy planner concerned with social services will not be able to avoid the investment-
consumption formulation in looking at proposals; but it is in the
very nature of social welfare, and therefore of social services, that
people of different value stances or time perspectives will classify
the same program differently and that in some cases one should
define investment in noneconomic terms. Particularly as human
gains or human benefits are included in the cost-benefit equation by which potential investments are evaluated, the boundary
between consumption and investment becomes very vague. On
the other hand, in the more extreme instances of developing countries or deprived areas or neighborhoods in developed countries,
the hard choices involved in allocating scarce manpower and
money may be helped by focusing on expected outcomes of competing programs. Then it may at times be useful to pose the issue
of "the program as an end in and of itself" or "the program as a
means toward a series of high-priority ends."

Public, Voluntary, and Proprietary

In today's terms policy issues relating to the roles of public, voluntary, and proprietary social services tend to be posed in one of the following forms:

1. Should voluntary (that is, nonstatutory) services be publicly funded?
2. Are there some categories of service that public agencies should not undertake?
3. How may or should public and voluntary agency services be interrelated at the operational level?
4. Should profit-making organizations be employed to deliver social services that, presumably, should be accessible to consumers whether or not they are able to command such services in the marketplace through their own resources?

These issues derive from historical context and are consequently different in the United States from what they are in the Mediterranean or South American countries, for example. Basic to the Protestant ethic (and thus the United States) is the idea that goodness cannot be legislated, cannot be compulsory. Laws may forbid or deter evil ("blue laws"), but good works are voluntary moral acts—thus, church-state separation, the emphasis on personal volunteering, the long hesitancy to allow government to involve itself in social welfare activity and the preference for nonpublic (voluntary, private, nonstatutory) social agencies.

When such agencies could not assemble needed resources, a tradition grew in some fields and in some places (child welfare, for example) permitting public subsidy. Public tax policy allowed a degree of credit for contributions to voluntary charities. Later, consumers-users of social services were given public vouchers that could be expended for voluntary agency services, even in profit-making organizations (rehabilitation and, then, nursing homes). Finally, following a pattern that had evolved in the industrial sector, particularly in connection with war industries, public funds might even be used to establish and capitalize a nonpublic agency (antipoverty corporations, hospital corporations). Should public money capitalize a profit-making social service? Inevitably, this was the next question.

A survey of the present pattern reveals historical residues

devoid of logic or policy guidance. Most institutions for the mentally ill are publicly operated, institutions for the dependent or
neglected child are heavily voluntary, but the foster home facilities are as likely to be public. Settlement houses and family service agencies are private, but neighborhood service centers are
public. Sometimes the auspice varies with the section of the
country, the historical period when the service began, extent of
sectarianism, or potential profitability of the undertaking (nursing
homes).

From a practical point of view, the welfare or service society,
which is an urban and industrial society, undertakes and requires
so large a volume of social services and develops so considerable
a rights component in its definition of entitlements (the "new
property"), that voluntary agencies cannot be conceived of as
meeting all needs by themselves. We have noted that voluntary
expenditures for general social services are only 15 percent of the
total, if that. The issue then becomes one of whether the public
agency should itself expend public funds for social services or
seek to use voluntary nonprofit (more accurately, nonpublic or
nonstatutory) or even profit-making agencies as public instruments.

In the United States, at least, it would probably be easier to
assure coverage, access, uniformity, accountability, and universality with relation to public social utilities and basic case services
if the access points themselves (see page 161) and some basic
services were publicly, that is, statutorily, operated—or at least
guaranteed. Planning, standard setting, licensing, and inspection
require a public base. There is certainly a place in each county for
a basic social service operation under government, with clear
recognition that this is a national pattern and that expectations are
definable.

Succinctly stated, this may seem like very little, but the paragraph above contains important implications. It affirms that only
public authority and sanction assure the possibility of developing
and enforcing standards over a large area. It accepts the premise
that service rights can be defined and guaranteed either through
public planning and operations or through careful contracting and
policing by the public authority. It recognizes that social services
are costly and that coverage can come only by means of support
from the public treasury. It notes that if public funds pay for the
bulk of a service, there is public obligation to spend money carefully—that is, to plan and to monitor the service or to deliver

service directly. It knows that, unless each governmental unit has an active public service outlet, probably at the county level, at least, in the United States, it cannot monitor services the public contracts for through the voluntary sector.

Beyond this, states, regions, and localities may face many options, with the parameters often definable on the federal level. That is, where federal funds are involved, as they are or will be in most major social services, the legislation will indicate whether the operation is to be public or whether local or state government (or, in some instances, Washington) may contract with nonprofit voluntary agencies or with profit-making groups to deliver service. Or, clients may be given cash or vouchers (food stamps, service "rights") to use in one or more types of outlets. Of late, federal legislation has been increasingly permissive, opening more options to the local level. Policy makers at the federal level are therefore continuously alert to this policy sphere, and local planners, legislators, and executives are engaged in major exploration of the subject.

Direct-service volunteering, of course, is possible in either publicly operated services (volunteer tutors in local schools) or voluntary agencies (child guidance escort volunteers or local committees that "adopt" institution cottages). The issue does not reside here. Pioneering and policy advocacy is found in either sector, too; the voluntary agencies have no monopoly or innovation or on pressing for client rights, despite the conventional wisdom, as any review of the last two decades of social service history will disclose. Nor is the voluntary agency truly autonomous, depending as it does on charters, referrals, subsidies, and tax-deductible contributions. Its role is susceptible to public policy making. Finally, consumer influence at the local level should be felt in both voluntary and public sectors.

By virtue of their nonstatutory status, voluntary services appear to have several unique possibilities. They might serve exceptional circumstances, where there is societal interest in doing things for individuals and groups that cannot be formulated as legal rights and made uniformly available (the family service agency that offers a major investment to put a family on its feet, the economic development agency that invests in one city neighborhood). Voluntary agencies are excellent vehicles, too, where what is needed is so venturesome and risky as to be unlikely for a politically responsible and sensitive group (the foundation that funds an unusual

consumer-interest enterprises, the agency that backs a controversial drug or family planning service).*

Most important, the voluntary service may assure *diversity*
even where there is public coverage—if diversity is valued. To
serve a complex country, or a heterogeneous local community, a
social policy may seek diversity in locus, staffing, philosophy,
and/or techniques. Commercial products on the market appeal to
a variety of tastes, and, while public services reflect some understanding of the needs of several types of consumers, the experience is that politically guided public services commonly must
forego some of the needed range for reasons of economy or caution. The voluntary here offers important flexibility.

Perhaps even more important is the fact that public services,
while they may offer religious outlets to individuals (as in the
instance of the prison chaplain, or the placement of a foster child
with a foster parent of a similar religion "if practicable"), cannot
have strong religious character. Otherwise, there would be the
claim that government is allowing itself to be used to "establish"
a religion. Yet there are people to whom religion is so critical a
component of daily life that, precisely under circumstances during
which they require social services, they wish sectarian services.
Family counseling, child guidance, adoption, maternity homes, residential treatment programs, and senior citizen centers often fit
into this category. This special kind of diversity, the agency offering the user a sectarian religious context reflecting cherished
values and cultural identity, is something that under our Constitution can be offered only by the voluntary agency, not by the public.

Beyond these well-defined roles, for which there is much his-

---

*Given political diversity and dispersion of authority among levels of govern-
ment, occasions have been created when public agencies took on the venturesome and the risky. Sometimes, as in the case of the antipoverty war of the
mid-1960s, this was even encouraged by Washington. It is in the nature of our
political system, however, that governmental programs may often be stalemated
and officials cannot take on high risks. It is at least helpful to have other
sources of support.

To some extent, the ability of public agencies to take risks is determined by
such things as whether different, but interacting, levels of government are under
the control of the same political party; whether officials on different levels,
whatever their party, are in rivalry; whether the program in question is a public
"whipping boy," and so on. Voluntary agencies, too, are subject to many idiosyncratic factors: board composition, source of voluntary funds (foundations,
United Way, endowment, investment, and so on), and nature of staffing.

torical experience, there is the fact that in the current anti-bureaucratic climate, in which many Americans strongly favor dispersion of power and fear increasing centralization and the proliferation of important service under governmental authority, the voluntary agency is also suggested and sometimes employed as a contractor to deliver a service that is a public responsibility. Whether as a semipublic corporation (antipoverty community corporation, New York City Hospitals Corporation) or as an autonomous agency, this entity undertakes a public role on a nonprofit or a cost-plus basis. It thus parallels the defense contractors, research and development corporations, or private professionals who have similar relationships to government in other fields. Here economy-efficiency criteria should obtain. When a new social service is to be launched, if there is no existing public instrument the planning agency might open the field for bids, while public programmers develop their own costs, too, on the basis of specifications that are circulated. If all other things are "equal"—that is, none of the above type conditions obtains, making nonpublic operation highly desirable—that agency should be selected—public, nonprofit, voluntary, proprietary—that offers the community the best buy.

Clearly, then, one can and should project a continuing contribution by the voluntary sector in the social service field in the United States. In addition, as will be seen in the discussion of vouchers and performance contracting, one could also envisage the entry of more profit-making suppliers of service, so that some of the advantages of the marketplace, insofar as they affect delivery efficiency and service effectiveness, may be tested in their application to this field. Scale and scope, constraints and limitations, nonetheless require definition for those who would plan ahead. For some, the overriding considerations are pragmatic: what pattern will assure diversity, responsiveness, economy? Here, experimentation and research are needed. For others, the issue of accountability is so central that they would permit voluntary development largely in the interstices of a basic public network. Still others see state-church issues and constitutional challenges as paramount: let the voluntary services, particularly sectarian services, develop insofar as citizens support and pay for them, but do not subsidize such services with tax funds and do not establish administrative patterns that allow users no real options and, in effect, coerce them into using voluntary outlets.

There are, too, those who believe that profit making negates key social service values; they cannot accept the notion that proprietary agencies belong on the team. Others prefer to look at the experience.

Wherever the dividing line is placed in the light of such considerations—and there is reason to expect a range of answers—the realization of the full benefits of the potential voluntary contribution will be dependent upon provision for coordination with the public sector. Social service guarantees need public affirmation; their translation into rights and benefits will depend on public implementation of planning responsibility.

General or Separatist Services*

In an earlier period this policy issue might have been formulated as "sectarian or nonsectarian programs," but the explosion of ethnic and racial separatism in the late 1960s requires a broader statement. Briefly, the issue is this: Granted that religious, ethnic, and racial groups have the right to establish and conduct social services for members of their own groups, and recognizing that these must be nonstatutory (voluntary) services, is it permissible or desirable for public funds or public tax policy to be employed to permit or even to encourage such separatism?

We shall not do full justice in this presentation to the legal issues, which are yet fully to be clarified in the courts with reference to their constitutionality. There has been some erosion of the principle of church-state separation as it relates to the issue of public subsidy of sectarian education. The vehicle for departure from traditional restrictions has been a strategy of aiding individuals rather than institutions, or of paying for facilities and equipment, not for personnel. Yet to be settled to the satisfaction of some members of the legal profession is the question of whether the long-time distinction between child welfare (substitute parenting) and education can be consitutionally sustained. For approximately a century there has been direct and indirect public support of, and even preference for, sectarian child welfare

*In some of the literature, the issue is phrased as "universal vs. particularistic services," but this creates confusion with universalism-selectivity, a distinction described above and referring to presence or absence of an economic means test.

services in some states, on the premise that this was not "establishment" of a religion.

The courts have held that the public may not finance a social service that discriminates against blacks, Mexicans, and other minority groups, even if government simultaneously funds a separate and similar program for such minorities. The "separate but equal" doctrine was discarded in the 1954 *Brown v. Board of Education* ruling of the U.S. Supreme Court. Not yet clear is how the courts will regard minority "discrimination" against majority group members or other minority groups in publicly funded programs. Can black or Hispanic or Indian separatist programs be legally sustained, or is the assumption that de facto separatism will simply develop and be tolerated because majority group members will not wish to utilize minority-run programs—even in areas in which so-called racial or ethnic majorities constitute a local minority? And will the courts also hold that de facto discrimination of this sort is also illegal for the minority, as it is for the majority?

These may appear to some as frivolous issues, but they are likely to be faced legally as the several racial-ethnic separatisms expand and as they dominate the scene in border areas and ghettos, where, in fact, some population elements will be deprived of service because of separatism. Even more often, one racial or ethnic minority group could by either deliberate or de facto discrimination based on separatist impulses be seriously depriving members of another—but legally weaker—minority.

Legal issues aside, the matter may be explored in a policy context focusing on value and factual components of the decision process. Historically, religious and ethnic minorities have developed their own social services in a spirit of mutual aid and also of self-protection because it was at times demanded of them if they wished to settle in specific colonies or cities. Social services have assisted acculturation and have introduced social control, often thus advancing the interests of an ethnic group. Such services have perpetuated or protected value components of culture and precious folkways; they have provided supports and continuity for individuals and families moving from the old to the new. Sometimes members of previously integrated groups have aided the newly arrived out of sympathy for their needs or to hasten their acculturation.

The program forms have varied with the basic objectives: centers and settlements for acculturation and preservation of old values as well; child-care services to protect group continuity; family services also as representing social continuity but facilitating the taking of aid because of shared experiences of the helper and the helped; boys' clubs as vehicles for value continuity and for supporting ethnic identification; and so on.

The very goals suggest the negative arguments. Separatism, if it stresses preservation and accentuation of differences rather than assuring a vantage point for integration in which valued differences are not considered as requiring separation, may be continually divisive and may even complicate social adjustment. In some instances it may deliberately encourage intergroup conflict. Moreover, the more advantaged ethnic groups do well by their "own," whereas those who are poor are frustrated even further. Redistributional goals may be thwarted by ethnically separated services, unless funded out of general revenues. Help is needed across ethnic lines and should not await individual magnanimity. Social service has redistributional possibilities and obligations that should not be ignored.

Resolution of the policy issues in this field remains difficult, since various participants in the debate apply different criteria. There is some evidence, for example, as in the Breiland Chicago child welfare study, of some consumer preference for racial identity of social service professional and client—but the degree of preference may be affected by the type of task and is modified when competence is introduced as a variable.[8] In sectarian services the specific nature of the service (marriage counseling, child welfare, group activity, education) may be of considerable importance to this issue.

Some people feel that consumer preference should not be the determining factor. What of broad public policy, such as integration? To those for whom separatism, integration, and pluralism may be the overriding legal or policy principles, questions of preference and effectiveness become secondary matters. Others, quite pragmatically, refuse to espouse a doctrine; they ask about the circumstances under which people in need are best reached and helped.

The issue is at the heart of current urban social policy debates and not readily resolved by social service planners alone. For those to whom black or Puerto Rican or Chinese or Japanese or Chicano separatism has become a major, new social goal, many of the traditional liberal social policy guidelines will fall. They will encourage separate services, segregated staffing, and public subsidy of it all, without needing to know if more people are actually better, or less satisfactorily, served as a result. For those espousing a liberal pluralism the emphasis will be on allowing the consumer-user maximum options and choices: public or voluntary service, sectarian and nonsectarian, unified and separated. They will probably back a basic public "coverage" service for most users, seeing such service as the vehicle for a public service guarantee and a prerequisite for planning, accountability, and case integration. At the same time, individuals preferring voluntary services, whether sectarian or racially or ethnically separatist, would be permitted to elect such service. This need not be difficult to arrange where services are financed out of insurance awards or by "vouchers" available to consumers by status or need. The issue encounters controversy as proposals are made for public purchase of care (less difficult) and subsidy (the most difficult issue). Here there is need not only for legal clarification, as proposed at the beginning of this section, but also some way to assure that the public purse is being employed to do what people want (diversity, choice, pluralism) and not to impose and induce preferences that are not prevalent (that is, giving a publicly supported monopoly to a separatist service whose main goals are political).

Finally, those to whom social solidarity is the cardinal principle will reject these rather pragmatic strategies and utilitarian rationales. While respecting individual freedom and difference they would not permit policies that undermine a society's integration. Thus, "there must be no allocation of resources which could create a sense of separateness between people. It is the explicit or implicit institutionalization of separateness, whether categorized in terms of income, class, race, color or religion, rather than the recognition of similarities between people and their needs which causes much of the world's suffering."[9]

NOTES

1. The classic and pioneering study is by Richard M. Titmuss, *Income Distribution and Social Change* (London: Allen and Unwin, 1962); see also his "The Role of Redistribution in Social Policy," *Social Security Bulletin*, 23, 6 (June 1965), 1–7. For the United States, see S. M. Miller and Pamela Roby, *The Future of Inequality* (New York: Basic Books,

1970); also, Herman Miller, *Rich Man, Poor Man* (New York: Crowell, 1971).

Robert J. Lampman has produced the most significant U.S. analyses thus far in "How Much Does the American System of Transfers Benefit the Poor?" in Leonard H. Goodman (ed.), *Economic Progress and Social Welfare* (New York: Columbia University Press, 1966), pp. 125–157, and also in "Transfer and Redistribution as Social Process," in Shirley Jenkins (ed.), *Social Security in International Perspective* (New York: Columbia University Press, 1969); see also his *Ends and Means of Reducing Poverty* (Chicago: Markham Publishing Co., 1971).

An international overview with specific reference to social services is found in United Nations, Department of Economic and Social Affairs, *Social Policy and Distribution of Income in the Nation,* ST/SOA/88 (New York: United Nations, 1969).

2. Miller and Roby, *The Future of Inequality,* Chapter 6.
3. *Social Policy and Distribution of Income in the Nation,* p. 15.
4. Alfred J. Kahn, "Perspectives on Access to Social Services," *Social Work* (London), 26, 3 (July 1969), 4; also in *Social Work* (New York), 15, 2 (April 1970), 97.
5. For a review of the tradition and an informed critique, Gunner Myrdal, "Investment in Man," constituting Chapter 29 of *Asian Drama* (New York: Pantheon, 1968), Vol. 3, 1533–1551. The American debate is illustrated in Martin Rein and S. M. Miller, "Poverty, Policy, and Purpose: The Dilemmas of Choice," in Leonard Goodman (ed.), *Economic Progress and Social Welfare* (New York: Columbia University Press, 1966), pp. 20–64, reprinted in Rein's *Social Policy* (New York: Random House, 1970), pp. 221–248.
6. Myrdal, "Investment in Man."
7. *Poverty Amid Plenty,* Report of the President's Commission on Income Maintenance Programs (Washington, D.C.: Government Printing Office, 1969), esp. pp. 74–75, 79–83.
8. Donald Breiland, "Black Identity and the Helping Person," *Children,* September–October 1969), 170–176.
9. Richard M. Titmuss, *The Gift Relationship* (New York: Pantheon, 1971), p. 238.

5

Policy
Meets Program

We have already noted the distinction between concrete services, such as day care or food stamps, and counseling or guidance. Some prefer to talk of these as "hard" and "soft" services. We have described the difference between money-granting programs of several kinds and general social services in our sense. We have yet to face the question of how one may formulate the choice between giving a person a benefit directly (food, an apartment) or giving him entitlements for the particular benefit he may "cash in" at one of a number of places (voucher) or providing him cash for the purpose—or for his own purposes. In short, we have yet to discuss one of the oldest policy questions in the social services field: "cash or benefits-in-kind?" It will soon become clear, as it has in the previous section, that policy options formulated as dichotomies or trichotomies are not necessarily resolved through absolute rejection of specified options. This discussion also serves to introduce a more fundamental question, already touched briefly in the previous section and to be approached in several ways in subsequent sections: To what extent and in what sense does the market and its mechanisms or concepts, in the economics sense, belong in the social services field?

Cash, Vouchers, or Benefits-in-Kind

To most people services are "concrete" things. Policy makers may debate the mix between "hard," practical services and counseling or guidance; but the question gains validity only as users, too, perceive the issue.

Genevieve Carter notes that studies of social services have shown consistently that users and potential users of social services in public welfare (generally very poor people) always list money as their first need and consider jobs and employment services as closely related to the money picture. Medical services are highest on the list of services, with assistance in getting money as the next priority. Poor people also see themselves helped (priority order) by having special needs granted (school clothing, housing equipment); being assured quick response in an emergency (check loss, child care during mother's hospitalization); by a social worker's intervention with landlords, teachers, police, and others who make major decisions affecting them; and by supportive referrals or procurement of resources such as food stamps, camps, Medicaid cards, and so on. There is far less recognition of counseling or advice about child care as service and little visibility for—if not negative response to—help with household management, parent-child relations, marital problems, and other issues involving personal change.[1]

The preferred listing does include what we have called liaison, access, and information services. Moreover, recognition of the need for personal help as service by a small percentage may imply significant case totals for a geographic area. Other studies show appreciation for interpersonal and behavioral help among persons higher in the economic scale—and when basic food and shelter needs have been met. Certainly, relationship and guidance should not be offered as substitute for or prior to food, shelter, medical attention, or clothing. But, when there is to be a benefit, whether concrete or relationship, the question remains as to how it should be conveyed to the user.

It has already been noted that services are part of the "new property." This does not relieve the policy analyst or the social services programmer of the need to consider when the provision of money is preferable to the guarantee of service, when service is preferable to money, or when vouchers are a desirable inter- mediary. Are vouchers, in fact, the equivalents of cash or of benefits-in-kind? The issues are as old as social services and the resolutions vary with societal concepts.

Several policy considerations are embedded in the general topic. Where the service is an indivisible good (clean air, a park, sewage disposal, a community center) no issue arises; the service cannot exist except as a benefit-in-kind created by the community, inde- pendent of consumer market behavior—even though user charges may be levied in some instances. Where real choice regarding means remains open—a circumstance for all but indivisible goods —there is, first, the matter of the better buy for the community. Where the policy planner can choose between cash or direct serv- ice, benefits-in-kind in the form of public social utilities or case services appear to enjoy the advantages of economy of scale. Although data are limited, it is a reasonable hypothesis that at a constant service volume, the benefit-in-kind approach is cheaper.

Public officials can buy food in bulk more cheaply than can a customer in a supermarket. Standard rental rates, negotiated en masse, are visible and (in the absence of corruption or gross inefficiency) likely to reflect the real market situation. (Besides, the cynical might add, benefit-in-kind products are often identifi- able, perhaps increasing stigma and decreasing applications. This was, after all, poor-law strategy.)

However, this issue is not simple. The inauguration of a benefit- in-kind may in fact increase the volume of provision under some circumstances. The unit cost may be cheaper but not the total expenditures. Whether the obsolete turkey basket for Thanksgiv- ing, the medical care program, the school lunch, there is some tendency, perhaps only in some fields, for grants of materials or services, rather than cash, to result in a quantitative increase in provision. It is not clear whether this is the result of service standardization (the recipient knows what to expect), organiza- tional dynamics (the administrators of a program increase their "customers" and thus their constituency), or the imposition of community rather than consumer priorities. Some benefit-in-kind services become near universal, or at least quite general in some areas; Medicaid services approached this situation in some parts of New York City in the early 1970s.

Thus, the issue is not resolved by reference to economy of scale and remains open to empirical exploration: Does benefit-in-kind provision increase or decrease volume of service? Do only specified types of benefits-in-kind lead to increased utilization? Do economies of scale really appear; if so, when? Do they balance increased demand?*

Opponents of benefits-in-kind have argued, usually, that whatever the specific case implications, social services are self-defeating if underprivileged members of the population are offered "in-kind" provision while everyone else utilizes cash. Here, then, is the heart of the matter. Whether focused on development-socialization or therapy-remediation, the purpose of the social service is to engender or to restore and enhance competence. If the recipient is given a "protected" benefit, that is, a service in kind, *in those instances where consumers in the free market would employ cash,* the agency is demonstrating "no confidence" and perpetuating dependency. Thus, when the country moved toward economic underpininng in certain circumstances after the Great Depression of the 1930s, social workers and others urged cash payments rather than food vouchers. It became and remains regressive social service practice in well-staffed agencies to offer Thanksgiving turkeys, Christmas baskets, food vouchers, or food stamps where people require and are perfectly competent to utilize cash. Indeed, benefits-in-kind in this sense—employed as a substitute for cash where the general consumer uses cash—are regarded as an avoidance of responsibility for adequate income maintenance.†

---

*Steiner documents low participation in food stamp programs, perhaps because of administrative requirements for regularity in purchase and for certain purchase minimums. Stigma also operates. Yet surplus commodity programs, involving more visibility and less consumer choice, have far higher participation in some circumstances. There is obviously much yet to be learned in this field. Gilbert Y. Steiner, *The State of Welfare* (Washington, D.C.: The Brookings Institution, 1971), pp. 193–213.

†Ibid. Steiner documents the unsatisfactory status of several benefit-in-kind programs in the United States in the early 1970s: surplus commodities, food stamps, public housing.

This is not to say that the phrase in the previous paragraph, "are perfectly competent," need be ignored by proponents of maximum use of cash. Dependent children need guardians. Some old people reach a point of requiring protection. There is considerable experience in the United States that, while abuse is possible, even cash assistance programs should have a procedure permitting "protected payments," where proven necessary (a third party handles the cash—or service could be offered, or categorical vouchers substituted). Benefits-in-kind are important for "less competent people"—meaning people who are found, through carefully specified procedures, incapable of managing money to purchase what is needed and spread it over the appropriate time horizon.[2] In all other instances one would favor cash where consumers in the free market, that is, people who do not ask for public aid, employ cash.

This rule of thumb does not settle all issues, however, for in a universalistic and rights context a benefits-in-kind approach would not need to involve stigma and might offer economy of scale and standardization of services. Public education is a prime illustration. Other illustrations are some health programs, libraries, cultural endeavors, and community centers. In a basic sense, a society's policies, as reflected in tax laws and other related legislation, as well as in collective bargaining agreements and wage policy, set the balance between wages and occupational welfare (including in-kind fringe benefits), between communal provision or communal goods and what the consumer must purchase for himself, and between cash and in-kind public entitlements. These are analyzable, debatable, and changeable decisions, although they do become somewhat fixed in community mores. To pose the issue of cash or benefits-in-kind in relation to universal services is therefore to seek for relevant anchor points.

A major consideration appears to be the degree of community determination that a specific service should be available to all and be utilized ("merit goods"). The presence of potential consumers, even consumers able to pay fees, is no guarantee that *enough* school or hospitals of the required *quality* will be made available. The technical "adequacy" of a parental budget does not assure that their children will purchase nutritious school lunches. In the 1960s, for example, housing for low-income people could not profitably be produced by the market; most education could not be paid for in a market economy. By creating a benefit-in-kind, suffi-

ciency and standards are, or could be, assured. Access may also
be improved. In addition, the program may be organized to achieve
universality, integration of population elements, and lack of divi-
siveness (for example, if *all* pupils eat lunch at school). This
arrangement avoids the problem of whether a consumer aided
financially will actually spend his resources to purchase the specific services deemed essential by the larger community.

Were communal benefit-in-kind provisions always accompanied
by automatic guarantees of sufficiency, quality control, and assured
access the issue here under discussion would seldom arise. However, both bureaucratic dynamics and communal factors creating
differential access by some population elements have challenged
these premises. Ghetto schools have been found inferior despite
formal legislative guarantees of equality or comparability. Professional interest groups and narrow constituencies have led institutions to avoid responsiveness to new circumstances and needs.
Bureaucratic rigidities and civil-service protections have nullified
efforts at quality control in communal services. As a result, increasing numbers of advocates from the left and from the right have
urged a departure from in-kind provisions and the assurance of
cash with which consumers may buy access to services. The proposals have related both to case services and to universal public
social utilities.

To illustrate, there are those who propose and continue to urge
that parents be provided with tuition money to purchase their
children's elementary and secondary education in the marketplace. The assumption is that competitive market forces will
enhance quality. In the housing field there has been some shift to
subsidy of the low-income renter and buyer (rent supplements,
mortgage supplements, and, most recently, housing allowances),
rather than the builder or public housing authority, to bring market components into the picture. Many health planners urge that
individuals be aided in purchasing health and hospital insurance,
as an alternative to a national health service.

To the charge that this approach leaves the naïve consumer
unable to judge quality, at the mercy of providers, the response is
that standard setting and inspection can and should be strengthened. Reference is also made to the fact that a "free market" and
its competitive forces, generate quality improvements. Again, we
must answer, "but only if the consumer can judge quality—something very difficult in education, medicine, counseling, and so on."

There is no escaping the need for improvements in enforced licensing, standard setting, and inspection. It is far from clear that a community or state not capable of organizing and implementing these essentials would be capable of carrying out successful and more economical direct service operations of its own.

To the point that the granting of money does not assure the desired pattern of expenditure by individual recipients, the proponents of "free markets" in welfare respond in two ways. First, as already noted, they assert that the consumer's judgment as to his family priorities should prevail—unless he is judged by the courts to be incapable of exercising family responsibility. Second, to the persistent rebuttal that a community has an obligation to define and protect access to some basic educational, health, and related services for all citizens, or at least for all children, whatever the personal judgments made, the idea of the categorical voucher is introduced. Medicare and vocational rehabilitation are cited as precedent.

A categorical voucher is thus definable either as benefit-in-kind (a way to provide a service the community deems essential) or as cash equivalent (the consumer may use it in the market and have the advantages of the competition generated by the bidding for his voucher). There have been numerous calls in recent years for systematic experimentation with vouchers for social services to see whether market dynamics might improve the quality and quantity of service. It has been proposed that nonprofit voluntary agencies, profit-making groups, and public agencies all be eligible to compete for the vouchers. As in the instance of cash, the naïve consumer with a voucher to spend will need some assurance that licensing, inspection, and certification arrangements protect him as he shops. There must also be provision to assure that a professional monopoly that is super-agency does not eliminate the benefits of competition that should accrue when competing agencies enter a market.

Apart from the issue of whether it is sound to use a voucher in a *particular* program (food stamps, for example) is the question of the extent of their use in a diversity of programs. Whereas it may be possible to make a case for vouchers in a specific context (housing or medical care or day care or education or prosthetic devices, and so on), the employment of vouchers for several different purposes at a given time and place would appear to infringe considerably on consumer autonomy and self-reliance.

In effect, the interim conclusion must be that the superiority of cash, voucher, or benefit-in-kind is contextual. It depends on a variety of community, agency, professional, and consumer factors that will vary with time, place, and milieu. Democratic values and many observations create a bias toward cash or vouchers, yet social realities and the real—if overrated—need to protect some people lean favorably toward benefits-in-kind. Each of the approaches can be made to work if the value hierarchies can be specified and the contexts analyzed. Conclusions vary, depending on whether the intent is to render a social service or conduct a publicly operated business.[3] This is a field in which scholars face several major research challenges.

The Performance Contract and Accountability

Market behavior provided one of the points of analysis of the "cash, benefits-in-kind, or vouchers" issue. The market and its dynamics are also cited in relation to another strategy that joins policy making with programming—the performance contract. It was enjoying faddest popularity as we went to press.

The performance contract is congruent with the economy-efficiency strategies of policy making (see page 125). It risks possible unplanned, unanticipated consequences and side effects to encourage service purveyors to emphasize output where others have been content with process. Social services, we have noted, have a history in charity and poor law. Intent, motive, and social control are their own justification in the tradition from which social welfare arises. Recipients belong to an underclass and should not raise too many questions about the quality of goods and services. It is such tradition that, when joined with the inherent complexity of the measurement and research "control" prolem, makes social service evaluative research so unsatisfactory— and rare.

The current era of operations research, PPBS, and consumerism has seen increasing challenges to this state of affairs: social service resources are scarce. The public should ask about effects and effectiveness. There is greater pressure for program evaluation that inquires not only about *process* (what does the professional do?) but also about *outcome* (what are the results of the doing?). If government would use the services of voluntary nonprofit or proprietary agencies, many who are concerned with output would urge that government pay fees for *delivered* (or effective) service, rather than grant general subsidies. Perhaps the consumer should pay directly when he knows the service has been delivered to his satisfaction even if he requires a publicly provided voucher for this purpose. In the instance of publicly delivered services, in this view, there should be routine output measures as a way to assure accountability: tests of the progress children make in their reading and writing, ratings of the cleanliness of city streets, statistics on criminals apprehended and convicted, reports on air quality, and data on consumer satisfaction with community centers or aftercare programs.

In this context, experiments with performance contracts have begun: an organization takes over an educational system with agreement that its compensation depends on the progress made by the children, as measured in specified fashion. Its "profits" depend upon successful "outputs" and not on "inputs" alone. Early reports are not impressive, but truly significant evaluation is not yet available.* While it is not likely that the practice will spread to many fields, there is much excitement about performance contracting as the route for escape from the alleged complacency of secure, salaried professionals who continue their established service modes without much attention to effectiveness. Indeed, enthusiastic proponents would lower the accountability one or two echelons and not pay teachers or other civil servants if children do not learn—arguing that teacher motivation is the critical variable.

Since there has been little social welfare experience with such approaches, an experimental posture toward performance contracts, as toward related market strategies, is justified. The dangers are visible and easily described: (1) Some performance contractors in education use operant conditioning strategies and reward the children for performance in turn (candy, trips)—the children learn skills but may not have balanced educational experiences. (2) If, in any program, there are agreed outcome variables that become the basis for payment, the specified goals may be achieved at the cost of many undesired side effects.

*However, in early 1972 the Office of Economic Opportunity (OEO) discontinued a major performance contract in elementary education because—after one year— the experiment did no better than traditional schools. Of course, logic might dictate dropping or continuing both!

If the performance contract approach is to persist, its advocates will need to demonstrate ability to develop acceptable criteria for success in service delivery. The measurement of a narrowly defined skill, while ignoring all else, will not be enough for most social services. But, of course, criteria for effectiveness must be formulated and measured whether or not there is to be performance contracting. Sophisticated outcome formulations and sound measurements should be possible where services have validity. The issue of whether the performance contract, per se, actually achieves better and cheaper results than other accountability approaches in the public services is an empirical one, worthy of exploration.*

Formalization vs. Participatory Administration

Most social services have been dominated by the professions and semiprofessions: medicine, education, social work, vocational rehabilitation, physical education, counseling, and so on. In recent years, the combination of ethnic separatism, interest in participatory democracy, and disillusionment with large organizations has created interest in decentralization and "community control" as vehicles to assure increased service responsiveness and improved quality. These forces have also encouraged interest in noncredentialed personnel and in less bureaucratized systems of organization and service delivery.

Decentralization as a programming strategy has implications for both more or less bureaucratized programs. However, when bureaucracies create local outlets without relaxing control, the term "dispersion" is more appropriate, since the outlets may all be cut from one pattern. There are exceptions, but a prerequisite of most authentic decentralizations is the offer of local options, to be exercised by staff or community (that is, less bureaucratization). We here consider one aspect, but a major aspect, of current policy approaches to greater program responsiveness: the search

---

*A "no-birth bonus scheme" currently being tested in southern India offers a "performance contract" of a sort to individuals. A tea picker who joins the scheme earns significant increments by avoiding pregnancy—under a "contract" developed by the United Planters' Association of Southern India, but implemented by plantation managements. *The New York Times,* July 2, 1972, p. 2.

for a balance between bureaucratization and what we would call "participatory administration."*

Most professionals (doctors, lawyers, and so on) do not work in bureaucratic organizations. In the general social services, however, they do. And the complaint is that rigid, formal organizational patterns shield staff from feedback, weaken consumers, and lead to organizational maintenance goals where there should be an emphasis on service to clients. The alternative posed, on the basis of the experience of recent years, is a locally shaped and controlled organization, with few guidelines and directives from higher levels, employing local people where possible, with local administrators (and/or line staff) hired by and subject to approval of "the community." Community control and decentralization become mutually reinforcing.

Others disagree. They would stress professional responsibility, competence, efficient organization, standardization, and accountability for funds. Thus emerges the policy issue: What balance is to be sought in development of a specific public social service between formalization, hierarchy, centralization, large organization, and economy of scale—on the one hand—and the variability, informality, uniqueness, experimentalism, and independence attributed to true community involvement and control—on the other?

Since evidence is limited and mixed, both as to whether the alleged attributes actually characterize community involvement and whether the advantages assumed really do follow, there is no empirical way to make the decision. Furthermore, the issue may be transitional or false, no matter how vital it may have seemed in the late 1960s. In a sense, the development of comprehensive services of any kind—day care, homemakers, individual help, substitute care, protective programs, or therapy—appears inevitably to lead to formal organization. Funding from higher to lower levels (most communities, especially poor communities, cannot fund their own social services), as well as standard setting and accountability, demand hierarchy for rule making and enforcement. Professional service requires layers of hierarchy for supervision and

---

*This section should be read in conjunction with the discussion of "general and separatist services" at the end of the previous chapter. On the limits of decentralization, a topic beyond the scope of this section, see Henry Cohen, "The Changing Role of the Planner in the Decision-Making Process," in Ernest Erber (ed.), *Urban Planning in Transition* (New York: Grossman Publishers, 1970), 180–181.

consultation. Diverse skills and specialties need to be meshed simultaneously and sequentially. Program units require policy coordination. Qualifications for various positions demand definition and publicization to avoid excessive nepotism, and promotional rules must be announced. Administrators cannot be held accountable unless they (rather than "the community") evaluate, hire, and fire. Reporting of several sorts, internal accounting, and various communication channels demand standardization.

In effect, social services tend to be professional activities of a special kind: unlike professionalism in the marketplace (private medical or dental practice, private law practice), social services generally are carried out in and through organizations. The normal dynamics of formal organization tend to generate the consequences described above, among others. Rather than bureaucratic "pathology," these developments may be defended as the vehicles for the objectivity, rationality, efficiency, and accountability that can be the contribution of modern organization. These latter impulses, in turn, tend to encourage consolidation and a search for both monopoly and economy of scale. Formal organization, thus, often becomes large-scale organization.

Why, then, the countertrends of the 1960s? Several factors appear to have operated. Initially, the issues of relevance and adaptability were raised. Were social services in deprived areas focusing on what was most needed, or on the processes of interest and priority to the agency staff? Were services taking adequate account of the life styles, cultures, predilections, concerns, modes of coping of consumers in deprived areas, particularly the poor, the ethnic and racial ghetto minorities? Could the professions continue to ignore evidence that people make more use of services that are close by? The case for diversity, adaptability, accessibility, and relevance became the case for decentralization. A pluralistic society, it was argued, could do no less.

Now the issue was escalated: First, the demand was made that organizations have local outlets and end the tendency toward large district or central offices. Smaller offices were proposed for natural neighborhood groupings, reflecting ethnic-racial-economic clusterings. Such offices would be more accessible, geographically and socially, and could reflect population diversities. Second, the call for decentralization and adaptability, a goal compatible with large-organization structure, since it could be met by a high degree of centrally directed "localization," was joined to a call for decen-

tralization of power, "community control." Here the objective
became political: The local group must control the local agency
if it is to be truly adapted to the program priorities and to the
service-using styles of the local residents.* A third ingredient was
also in the picture, the "new careers" emphasis on employment
within local social services of indigenous paraprofessionals—both
to assure service responsiveness and to create jobs for the poor.

Some observers see the political demand for community control
and employment of local paraprofessionals as the natural consequence of the neighborhood need to assure its own program priorities and delivery modes. Others believe that the political
objectives came first and that the program rationale has been used
to bolster the case. Since one may cite illustrations of each type,
it is probably true that the community control and staffing demands
of the late 1960s stemmed from both sources. There was no firm
empirical basis for either argument as the demands shifted from
education to health, mental health, and public welfare in the late
1960s. However, the issue had become so salient that no new
programming could be seriously considered without attention to
the question—at least insofar as poverty areas were concerned.

Political jockeying about community control may long confuse
the social service policy issues. But the political decisions will be
made in terms of stakes and factors that go well beyond the social
services. We assume that American society, or any large, interdependent nation, cannot frequently, consistently, and in many
fields reject the position that Lincoln took in his rebuttal to Doug-
las: the sacred right of self-government of the few cannot be
permitted to override the concerns of an entire nation. A sensitive
nation, however, will wish to employ decentralization, sometimes

---

*Advocates of community control and of the employment of indigenous person-
nel implicitly reject Banfield's analysis and its alternative policy implications. It
should be recalled that early Head Start programming emphasized cognitive
deficits of children reared in "culturally deprived" environments. To remove
them from such environments was to open new opportunity. Banfield argues,
along similar lines, that the urban problem is the problem of a social underclass
and that theoretically the most effective intervention would require separation of
"lower class" (which he distinguished from "working class") children from parents and environment. We might extrapolate from this a policy that favors domi-
nation and staffing of institutions serving lower-class children by working and
middle-class boards and professional personnel. This is quite contrary to American social policy of the past decade. See Edward C. Banfield, *The Unheavenly
City* (Boston: Little, Brown, 1970), esp. Chapters 3 and 11.

as local control and antiformalization, and sometimes merely as service localization, when comprehensive analysis of its interests suggests it. There can be neither a fully centralized nor a fully decentralized strategy.* Social service planners will wish to identify those program types or *social situations* that require far more flexibility, adaptability, unorthodox staffing, and community involvement than is possible for the local outlet of a centralized service. In such instances, funding mechanisms and accountability devices must be sought or invented that will allow the maximum of program decentralization, community control, and staffing experimentation. Such programs would avoid excessive formalization and structuring and would be small enough to carry it off. Most programs can tolerate more standardization than this, while allowing for adaptability and localization (that is, decentralization without community control, or what is called "administrative," as opposed to "political" decentralization). In many programs the technology is quite standardized or the options scientifically engendered (health services, employment placement, public assistance). Often the outcome variables are standardized and measurable (secondary education). Generally, higher levels of government have a commitment to legislative bodies about the quantity or quality of service that is being offered and for assurance of its delivery without the imposition of additional requirements on local citizens (separatism, participation). We may therefore expect that formalization and bureaucratization will continued in social services, as in most modern enterprises, despite consciously protected exceptions. What is also to be expected, however, is that *organizational* solutions will be sought for many of the problems that do seem to

---

*A rigorous analysis shows that no central body can survive without information; and information, in turn, is never fully separate from authority. This sets parameters on decentralization, according to Julius Margolis, "Decentralization and Urban Problems," in Anthony H. Pascal (ed.), *Thinking About Cities* (Belmont, Calif.: Dickenson Publishing Co., 1970). However, local variability and complexity demand some degree of decentralization, Margolis adds, arguing for a mixed system. Many authors caution that the decentralized decision-making bodies are more often than not oriented toward land values, not "population" values—or fail for other reasons to deliver the desired, responsive services. See Irving Kristol, "Decentralization and Bureaucracy in Local Government," in Pascal (ed.), ibid, pp. 69–80, or "Decentralization for What?" in *The Public Interest*, 11 (Spring 1968), 17–25. See also Howard Hallman, *Neighborhood Control of Public Programs: Case Studies of Community Corporations and Neighborhood Boards* (New York: Praeger, 1971).

flow from the bureaucratization process as it affects social welfare, such as complexity, case discontinuity, lack of accountability, disappearance of diversity, and decline of consumer initiative and responsibility. Some of these matters are discussed in the final section of this book, where programming is emphasized.

Finally, we might predict that the issues—decentralization, local control—will be with us as long as there are closed-out groups or consumers who consider services unresponsive and inflexible. The demand for what we have called "participatory administration" will recur as long as organizational maintenance seems to dominate service delivery. A satisfied consumer will find higher priorities on his time than the monitoring and "control" of local social services. Even where his is the formal control (the suburban school board), he will under most normal circumstances delegate responsibility to administrators—whom he can remove for poor performance.*

Policy Choices by Efficiency Rating

Many economists and political scientists would find the discussion to this point quite incomplete or even irrelevant. The policy issues posed involve various combinations of value choices and empirical assumptions. Except where market strategies were referred to (vouchers, performance contracts) there has been little attention to the actual review, within the decision process, of data regarding economy and efficiency. Yet much of policy analysis in other fields gives highest priority to these latter considerations.[4]

Thus, a debate about income maintenance strategy is resolved by a federal commission and by other analysts on the basis of expert research that shows that—if efficiency is defined in its economic sense as involving the proportion of expenditure reaching the "target population," the poor—negative income tax approaches are more efficient than family allowances.[5] No weight is given in the final debate to the universalism-selectivity considerations and the fact that means-test approaches may stigmatize while universal methods reinforce "solidarity."[6]

The same analysts, we have noted, argued against expanded public day care as part of a reform of public assistance on the

*Twenty-five years ago this section would have discussed another policy question: client self-determination versus control. See Alan Keith-Lucas, *Decisions About People in Need* (Chapel Hill: University of North Carolina Press, 1957).

grounds that the payoff was too small—it would cost more to provide good day care than the mothers could earn. Family planning services, on the other hand, yielded high cost-benefit ratios and were readily recommended for expansion in another study.

In short, operations research, cost-benefit studies, and other quantitative policy-analytic techniques ask questions about efficiency and economy. They employ the tools of decision theory or of the market expert. Sometimes their conceptual point of departure is welfare economics.[7] This class or family of methods has begun to enjoy increased respectability among social service planners and policy makers as pressure has increased for better results and more efficient use of resources. Where resources are in short supply objective evidence is asked about the payoff potentials of competing opportunities for expenditure or investment. The very pressures that have pushed governments toward program budgeting and PPBS[8]—approaches that require cost-benefit analysis—have thus also encouraged use of efficiency criteria in other policy-making circumstances.

The potential or helpfulness of such methods is hardly to be questioned. One collection of reports, randomly selected, for example, shows how rigorous, analytic, often quantitative research related to decision options could contribute to decisions about:

1. Warehouse centralization for public supplies
2. Routing of vehicular traffic
3. Urban renewal programming
4. Assignment of telephone-information agents
5. Determining bed capacity and nursing staff for a hospital
6. The expansion of community-based treatment for specified categories of offenders[9]

Review of these and other studies also discloses that this family of methods (operations research, systems analysis) *does not yet involve one standard set of procedures.* The studies are characterized by specification of goals, careful attempts at quantification, specification of alternatives available, clear definition of criteria, and the employment of either "best buy" for a given expenditure unit or "cheaper price" for a given desired effect as the decision-making base.

Why, then, the discussions of policy options in the earlier chapters? Why the value and preference debates we have summarized?

Why not an expansion of operations research and cost-benefit studies as the *sole* strategy to improve policy making? Alice Rivlin has summed up her experience as assistant HEW secretary in charge of planning and evaluation at a time when there was an "all-out" governmental attempt to introduce analytic quantitative thinking, cost-benefit studies, and PPBS:

First, such approaches can and do produce useful, quantitative answers to such questions as what the problems are, how they are distributed, and in whom they reside.

Second, such approaches can and do add considerably to the knowledge of who might be helped by specific programs and at what cost (who benefits and who pays?).

But, third, such analytic work, in the absence of application of other values or political considerations, cannot tell one how to choose among programs with different objectives (developmental services for young children, community centers for the aged).

Nor does such work, per se, tell the planner how to improve services.[10]

Rivlin found, as had Charles J. Hitch, who introduced much of the federal government to PPBS, that "systems analysis is simply a method to get before the decision maker the relevant data, organized in a way more useful to him." She also concluded, with her predecessor, William Gorham, that analytic methods like cost benefit do not shed light on the large program options and on balancing the investment among a variety of public objectives, since legislators and members of the executive branch prefer to trust their political intuitions above cost-benefit ratios derived from debatable assumptions. However, as Gorham has noted, once the large choice is made, programming decisions within a given field or project can (or should) be improved through such analytic work. The systems analyst cannot help one to decide between more elementary school educational support or more investment in manpower programs. After a selection is made, he can help choose among programs or specify details within the selected field.

The efficiency approaches may sometimes shed light on the consequences of choosing decentralization or centralization; vouchers or benefits-in-kind or cash; universal or selective strategies. They can specify the costs or benefits of funding voluntary programs, as opposed to public operations. The decision maker will—or should—therefore seek out program analysts and operations researchers. To the extent that evidence of an objective kind, derived from economic premises, can be helpful, he obviously cannot ignore such evidence. We have suggested in the above earlier discussions of policy options where it would be particularly helpful to have objective data of particular kinds, relevant to choices.

And even where assessments of political realities or dominant value configurations introduce forces that are critical to the decision making, the objective, analytic data about costs and benefits are essential. Decision makers need to know the real price of a value preference, a popular demand, or a political requirement. Perhaps cost will at times sway the decision, outweigh a pressure. If not, the more costly or less efficient choice should at least be knowingly made. It can, perhaps, be consciously faced as an essential trade-off, and should condition expectations as to program outcome.

Ultimately, of course, it must become clear that in specified circumstances some of the "other value" oriented options can or should be adopted with full understanding that they contradict or are in tension with efficiency approaches. Arnold Gurin has noted this recently. In an analysis of a variety of social service policy issues he points out that sometimes efficiency criteria will lead to the choice of service unit sizes and geographic boundaries for programs that negate the push (from other value perspectives) for greater decentralization, as a contribution to increased democracy.[11] Gurin does not make this a firm, universal generalization, but notes that it *may* hold in some circumstances, thus illustrating the tension between the efficiency criterion and others. Similarly, amidst the rush toward decentralization he notes that "considerations of equity lead inevitably toward centralization." Only central initiative and power can assure coverage, resources (fair quantity), and standards—the preconditions of equity.

Bauer and his collaborators have also shown how "economizing," if this is taken to mean the various policy development models in normative economic theory, may be in tension with other value hierarchies and/or may be differently interpreted and employed as other values are introduced. A project may be worth undertaking, for example, given zero results in cost-benefit efficiency if it nonetheless has redistributional impact. Administrators and policy board members may wish to reject choices that would appear to follow from market-efficiency models because other values are dominant.[12] Participation, especially the variations on "maximum feasible participation," has a pace and reaches conclusions that are often in tension with, or even quite opposite from, those derived from operations research and cost-benefit studies.[13] There is a convergence (Bauer) that states that although people have more complex approaches to utility preference than does a market-efficiency model, the decision maker has need to know what the efficiency approach has shown. Furthermore (Stokes), since "analytical skills are for sale," community participation in its more sophisticated stages may employ analysts who share the "other" values that are central both to monitor the output of governmental planning and to develop plans and proposals in areas where the locality makes the decisions.

In introducing the problem of tension among policy options, we arrive at the question of whether there is an identifiable hierarchy among them. Are there some choices that should always be made first? Do some decisions lead to resolution of a broad range of issues? Is there a general paradigm that orders these and related policy issues and that is applicable to all or most social service policy matters?

The Lack of a General Paradigm

The answer is simple, direct, negative. Nobody can offer one well-developed social policy paradigm, proven in its applicability to all decision making in social services. Nor is it clear that a paradigm will or should evolve. Some of the dimensions outlined appear to have greater weight at one moment than at another. Any hierarchy that is established among the choices is contextual, or dependent upon both reality assessment and a balancing among values. One cannot announce which questions must always be settled first or how a decision about one policy issue should influence decisions about others. The issue hierarchy shifts with general fluctuations in preference and in power of competing decision makers and with changing times. Economizing or optimizing models lead in one direction, social welfare or "sociologizing" in another.*

---

*Martin Rein illustrates in detail how the policy analyst's ideology and values affect his assessment of policy process, policy research, and the hierarchy of policy dimensions. This extends to the weighing of economy-efficiency and of other policy targets. See "Social Policy Analysis as the Interpretation of Beliefs," *Journal of the American Institute of Planners*, 37, 5 (September 1971), 297–310. See also reference to Bell on page 73.

Nevertheless, students of social services have increasingly been able to conceptualize their roles in society and to clarify the potential consequences operationally and philosophically of different choices from among the options. And reporting of experience and employment of an understandable vocabulary about social service policy matters does sharpen issues and permit decision makers to act with far more insight than ever before into the significance and potential consequences of what they do.

In short, while the social service programmer or policy maker does not have access to clear operational rules for selection among all the following options, nor is it clear that all are relevant in all circumstances, he is less likely to proceed blindly if he is acquainted with the thinking and experience relevant to consumption-investment; formal organizational structure–participatory administration; redistributive–not redistributive in primary goal; public social utilities–case services; "rights" or non-rights basis of entitlement; general or separatist services; cash, vouchers, or benefits-in-kind; public-voluntary services—and so on. Many of these issues and several others that they suggest are translatable into general programming strategy or detailed operational guidelines.

A final word about policy: ideally, policy choices are based on an exploration of their empirical and value consequences and analysis of their compatability with other strongly held values and goals. The premise therefore always is that if one adopts the given policy, certain desired consequences will follow. Some of the assumptions may not be correct; research would be useful in this connection. Often, policy choices are made in the belief that specific policies implement favored values, yet the empirical base for the assumption proves to be flimsy. Are decentralized services truly always more responsive to local priorities and better able to adapt delivery system to subgroup circumstances than centralized programs? Is it true that, in many fields, means-tested programs are stigmatized and have more trouble in assuring quality of program than universal programs? Do the assumed advantages accrue to consumers who can spend money for services in the marketplace, as contrasted with those who must utilize publicly provided services "in kind"? Do so-called "investment"-type social services pay off for societies that are modernizing more rapidly than do "consumption" programs? Does "community control" enhance program responsiveness? Does selectivity increase or decrease "take-up," add to or diminish disincentives?[14]

Dimensions usually discussed separately may be or are in tension: equality and decentralization, integration and decentralization, efficiency and local "control" or subsidization of small voluntary agencies. These, too, are matters for further analysis and research. A decision maker cannot forgo full understanding of where his choices may lead. Therefore, there is need for more case studies of the policy correlates of various choices in social service, with special focus on the interrelations among the dimensions discussed in the past several chapters.

The efficiency-economy "school" of policy analysis cannot be excluded from this exploration. Premised on the notion that "least cost," "best buy," "greatest efficiency" are high or highest values, such approaches eventually must be absorbed into the decision process in a political environment that may at times give equal or higher priority to other value perspectives. Here, too, then, there is need to study and examine the interplay among efficiency and some of the other values posited by those who debate policy questions. Policy analysis cannot be assigned completely to operations research, but is obviously impoverished without it. Nor can social workers and others merely proclaim rejection of efficiency approaches while adopting "other" stances—unless they do more to elaborate and clarify their unique orientations.

The policy issues discussed earlier in this section do not comprise the universe of possibilities. When values confront social realities in a given historical context there are many dilemmas. At a given moment, particular issues enter the debate as matters of high policy. Special attention has therefore been directed at choices currently highlighted in the social services. Others will seem more urgent, at other times; any particular paradigm will be short-lived.

Related to the major policy items are others which are intermediate between high policy and programming strategy. Elsewhere I have called these "parameters of programming."[15] For example, a provision about the degree of centralization-decentralization might help in choices about assignment of program operations to a given level of government, one of the intermediate policy questions. A decision about rights would require specification of type of accountability mechanism. Efficiency criteria would mandate choices in favor of provisions for case integration and responsibility.

A clear goal relative to redistribution could provide guidance in specifying program benefits and the method of financing. The latter issue would also be helped toward resolution once there is a point of view about introduction of or freedom from market strategies in social welfare programs.

For a given purpose, a policy frame must be developed. The social planner or policy scientist (the term varies with the analytic model) cannot ignore the issue of policy coherence, lest what begins as policy clarification emerges as policy "sprawl." This means, in turn, some clarity about task or goal, empirical and value "screens," political assessment, and enough projection of alternatives and their consequences to discover both complementarities and tensions. In short, while there are no always-relevant and ever-transferable paradigms, the analyst does not choose policy parameters, one at a time, and by instinct. Societies, on all their institutional levels, are complex interdependent systems. This, too, cannot be ignored.

NOTES

1. Genevieve W. Carter, "The Challenge of Accountability—How We Measure the Outcomes of Our Efforts," *Public Welfare,* 29, 3 (Summer 1971), 271.
2. For a rationale for employment of benefits-in-kind for the "incompetent poor" on a relatively large scale see Edward C. Banfield, *The Unheavenly City* (Boston: Little, Brown, 1970), p. 246 and Chapter 6. Banfield feels that cash harms those whose poverty has "inward" causes since it maximizes disincentives.
3. Gilbert Y. Steiner, *The State of Welfare* (Washington, D.C.: The Brookings Institution, 1971).
4. For example, see Raymond A. Bauer and Kenneth J. Gergen, *The Study of Policy Formation* (New York: Free Press, 1968); Anthony H. Pascal (ed.), *Thinking About Cities* (Santa Monica, Calif.: Rand Corp., 1970); Joseph A. Kershaw, *Government Against Poverty* (Chicago: Markham Publishing Co., 1970); Philip M. Morse (ed.), *Operations Research for Public Systems* (Cambridge, Mass.: MIT Press, 1967). An evaluative review of experience in the Department of Health, Education, and Welfare is offered by Alice Rivlin in *Systematic Thinking for Social Action* (Washington, D.C.: The Brookings Institution, 1971). Or see recent issues of such journals as *Policy Sciences* or *Journal of Human Resources* for illustration.

5. *Poverty Amidst Plenty,* Report of the President's Commission on Income Maintenance Programs (Washington, D.C.: Government Printing Office, 1969).

6. Alvin Schorr, *Poor Kids* (New York: Basic Books, 1966).

7. Richard Zeckhauser and Elmer Shaefer, "Public Policy and Normative Economic Theory," in Bauer and Gergen, *The Study of Policy Formation,* pp. 27–102; or, for an illustration, see Kenneth Arrow, "Criteria, Institutions, and Function in Urban Development Decisions," in Pascal (ed.), *Thinking About Cities.*

8. Alfred J. Kahn, *Theory and Practice of Social Planning* (New York: Russell Sage Foundation, 1969), Chapter 8.

9. Philip M. Morse (ed.), *Operations Research for Public Systems* (Cambridge, Mass.: MIT Press, 1967).

10. Paraphrased and summarized from Rivlin, *Systematic Thinking for Social Action.*

11. Arnold Gurin, "Responsiveness and Control of the Social Services: Some Issues of Decentralization," unpublished lecture, 1970. Adams argues that "purely economic solutions will not do. Yet, the economic value set is likely still the best place to begin a policy analysis . . . by starting with economic values and a production model, he [the policy analyst] can often . . . 'flush out' the professional values and goal structure . . . ." This case illustration deals with rehabilitation. See Harold W. Adams, "On Economic Values in Policy Analysis," *Policy Science,* 1, 2 (Summer 1970), 214.

12. Raymond A. Bauer, *Social Indicators* (Cambridge, Mass.: MIT Press, 1966), pp. 71, 113.

13. Geoffrey C. Stokes, "Maximum Feasible Participation Confronts New Management," *Trans-action,* 8, 11 (September 1971), 4–10.

14. On the latter, see Mike Reddin, "Universality Versus Selectivity," in William A. Robson and Bernard Crick (eds.), *The Future of the Social Services* (Baltimore: Penguin, 1970).

15. Kahn, *Theory and Practice of Social Planning,* pp. 208–211.

Programs

The Programming
Model Reflects a Policy

The citizen or the public official must not withdraw from the policy exploration at the level of high abstraction. If he would influence programs as they enact policy and would monitor output from the perspective of policy goals, he must also consider the relationship between policy and program. These final sections are devoted to the topic; but, since research into policy consequences and complementarities is limited, one can say little that is firm. Much of what follows his face validity, at most. Much of it poses research tasks, but cannot rest on research evidence.

While there is some inevitable tendency in these chapters to be prescriptive, the objective is to introduce analytic habits for those who do or should care about the interplay of policy and program. The materials are deliberately fragmentary and illustrative. The concern with policy alertness would be lost were we to offer a complete manual of social service administration or a checklist of policy guides.

Interested citizens and public officials should know that the social service administrator or program planner finds some of the policy choices outlined in the previous section relatively clear-cut; his implementation mission is then not ambiguous. A program may be public or voluntary; federal, state, or local; sectarian or nonsectarian; more or less decentralized in administration; financed one way or another. There may be many details to be worked out, regulations to be formulated, organizational structure to be designed. Yet the nature of the choice to be made is specified in the policy issue, and its operational referents are identifiable in practice.

Other policy issues are far less readily translated into program specificity. For example, when we go beyond a decision to assign a program to either the public or the voluntary sector and express a preference for a "mix," complex questions of quantity, coordination, client rights are introduced. The solutions may advance or undercut basic objectives. Or a decision to add flexibility and options, where a basic program structure is legislatively specified and bureaucratized, faces the administrator with many decisions that can, in effect, make new policy.

The complexity involves more than just developing details where there are only objectives or direction. Since policy thrusts are often chosen because of their assumed compatibility with overall political goals or value stances, their empirical basis may be meager. The formal policy choice does not in itself imply clarity as to how it is to be implemented. The programmer may find it necessary to experiment with alternate means to realize a policy or may choose the most likely route and monitor it carefully. For example, a universal social utility demands a series of easy entry points and the planner must provide them, without knowing whether the particular scheme set up actually achieves general access. Any attempt to use social services for redistributional objectives must be quite experimental, since a series of unknowns about access, utilization rates, alternatives as defined by consumers, and so on, are at stake.

None of this is easy, since the charity derivations of many of the social services and the close relationship of many general social services to religious and humanitarian programs with long tradition assure that any programming effort begins with a large component of conventional wisdom and what might be called conventional practice. An act of will and a spark of creativity is often required to appreciate that the intended program does not carry with it an "obvious" and "clearly appropriate" approach and that it is useful to pause to consider the means by which policies may be most effectively realized.

As he thinks about implementation, the program developer or administrator has the following among his reference points:

1. General or "high" policy objectives
2. Values and standards that are dominant in our ethic
3. Administrative principles
4. Experimental strategies

And he operates in a highly political environment. In addition, to facilitate his intellectual tasks and administrative activities, he is offered systems of concepts that would organize the relevant variables and sharpen his choices. Those who care about policy do well to note that even the choice of a model has consequences. Especially relevant to social services, and not necessarily always mutually exclusive, are:

1. Public health conceptualizations
2. Systems approaches
3. Market strategies
4. The concept of network (a "partial system")

Public Health Conceptualizations

Public health concepts have been very useful to social service programmers over the years, particularly as they have concerned themselves with case services. Some elaboration of public health concepts is needed for this purpose, but the approach has proven merit.[1]

Public health theory and practice have been developed on the basis of early preoccupation with three elements: *agent, host,* and *environment.* Traditionally, prevention consists of eliminating agents (eradicating the mosquitoes), strengthening the host (immunization and general health measures), and improving the environment (putting up a screen, draining swamps). Treatment, in turn, requires detecting those infected, preferably early, and eliminating the disease from the host. Rehabilitation involves maximizing functioning of those affected, whose treatment would not completely eliminate the condition but who can benefit from retraining, prosthetic devices, and encouragement.

For reasons not immediately relevant, public health personnel have developed a rhetoric of "prevention" to describe such activities: primary prevention (changing the environment, strengthening hosts, eliminating agents), secondary prevention (early detection and cure before there is impairment), tertiary prevention (treatment), and rehabilitation. The concepts have been refined and their use improved by the addition of epidemiology (study of distribution of pathology in the environment), the recognition that health is more than the absence of disease and is probably part of another continuum, and the insight that treatment and rehabilitation often require positive "inputs," not merely the counteracting of agents and of negative factors.

Notions of this sort (grossly oversimplified above) have been of considerable use to organizers of social services: prevention, treatment, and rehabilitation have been differentiated and have often been assigned to different agencies and personnel. When there is individual, family, or group trouble, it is "diagnosed," so that a focused treatment or rehabilitation plan may be made. Much of the medical delivery scheme has been translated into social service analogues: inpatient and outpatient services, diagnostic process, treatment unit, general practice and specializations, patterns of treatment, and social worker–client relationship.

Three types of limitations have been noted:

1. For all its talk about prevention, public health tends to be oriented to pathology. Environmental improvements are considered in relation to avoiding illness; the "medical model" of intervention targets in on "disorder." The theory of enhancement of functioning is poorly developed, since public health people are basically expert clinicians undertaking a broader mission than the individual doctor. For social service programmers this is a serious problem, since most public social utilities are inventions intended for universal access. They seek to enrich communal living and to promote individual development and socialization. They need a broader framework than the mere avoidance of pathology.

2. The public health model works best where the problem concerns contagion. Public health conceptualizations applied to social situations may tend to overdo the disease and contagion analogy, with the result that victims are blamed ("Why didn't they practice good hygiene or avoid the bug?") or isolated ("Let us not permit it to spread."). Public health thought patterns in international rela-

tions led to the concept during the 1930s that international crises could be resolved by "quarantine [of] the aggressor."

The social service planner deals in his case services with acute conditions and also with states and conditions that are dysfunctional for the victim but "normal" to the system (poverty, relative deprivation, personal incompatibilities, and so on). He needs a broader model of intervention lest he try to cope with all societal malfunctioning by treating victims.

3. Whereas in some social services it may be useful to think of the service "event" as social worker treating or helping a client (doctor-patient relationship), this model of service may be dysfunctional for other social service realms where the issue may be one of the following: (a) access to a concrete service in which the worker is an intermediary but not an agent of personal change; (b) self-organization for mutual aid; (c) staff and users together seeking answers not known at the outset to the practitioner (some urban community development, for example). For social services often deal with problems for which there are no "answers" in the sense of scientific "cures," but actions based on group interests and preferences. For example, community control and client participation in decentralized services create dynamics inconsistent with rational implementation of a public health model, which suggests the linear sequence—diagnose-treat-cure.

One concludes with the view that public health approaches and categories are useful for alerting the administrator and planner to some issues and programming possibilities, particularly in relation to case services; but they need to be supplemented by other concepts, particularly if case services are not the focus or the sole focus. Even with regard to case services, where the medical model is at its best, there is need for inventive adaptation to the general social service context so as to take account of the following: social service components are less clearly interrelated than medical specialties; more social services carry stigma, are "protective"; there are patterns of competition and overlapping among professions and agencies rendering services; there are aspects of poor law and charity heritage that complicate the service design; sectarian and voluntary services carry much of the responsibility in some parts of the country and in some fields, but not in others; public information and acceptance of social services and social services expertise do not compare with public searching out of medical services for many conditions.

Systems Approaches

A public health approach is a form of systems analysis. Systems approaches are analytic planning efforts that seek to take account of the range of major interacting variables relevant to the field in focus. In general, because of the number of factors deemed relevant and the complexity of relationships, research application for such approaches have become possible only as computers have become available.

For present purposes, there is no need to clarify the several meanings of systems analysis.[2] Among the major ideas here relevant are the following:[3] A variety of components are interrelated, by some connective force, so that performance of one component is affected by performance of another component. By studying such relationships, learning how the system is influenced, and arranging for signals (feedback) from components, it is often possible to exert a measure of control. The control is oriented to the "big-picture payoff," in Boguslaw's terms, that is, the goals chosen for the system, rather than to performance of components, except insofar as the latter are oriented to the former.

The policy maker may choose a systems approach because it is essential to effectiveness-efficiency, a way to be most responsive, or a planful way to interrelate many elements (public-voluntary). Or he may choose a systems perspective because those who observe his performance do. To quote Rivlin:

. . . the history of the Family Assistance Plan also illustrates another point about analysis: the importance of looking at the whole problem rather than just a piece of it. In developing the Plan the analysts had enough problems handling the interrelations between the old welfare system, Family Assistance, the tax system and food stamps. They appear literally to have forgotten that some other income-tested benefits were available to the poor, such as public housing, rent supplements and Medicaid. When these other programs were brought into the picture it turned out to be at least theoretically possible for a family on Family Assistance to lose all monetary incentive to work. Such a family might be better off on assistance than working for higher wages and losing their income-related benefits. This spectre, raised in the Senate Finance Committee, sent the Administration analysts back to their computers to devise a more comprehensive proposal that would preserve incentives to work.[4]

The systems approach is organic, yet avoids false organismic analogies. Total situations are to be characterized and overall goals and directions kept in mind. Yet, in a sense, at some levels, all things are parts of systems involving larger things, so there is a degree of arbitrariness in deciding what to include, where to stop. The real world sometimes sets the limits: a city may operate elementary and secondary schools, but not colleges; a state may be responsible for juvenile institutions, but not youth police. If not faced by political or legal systems definitions initially, the planner must seek them out in relation to what he wishes to achieve and what is conceptually sound. He considers medical care, recreation, housing, education, and so on, as operating systems and stops to ask whether it is conceptually wise and politically feasible to join them—or some of them—with welfare and manpower in a human services system, for example.

The application of a systems approach (and operations research) to a local government's social service decision making is illustrated by the following summary and flow chart.[5] (See Table 4 and Chart 1.) It will be noted at once that the relatively arbitrary decision to exclude voluntary parental placement and many adoptions, the failure to address prevention strategies, the elimination of income maintenance as an approach, and the questionable assumption that volume of need would remain unchanged, all add up to a considerable compromise with the systems concept. Occasionally (see the quote from Schon on page 146) there is a comprehensive approach, although action recommendations are then only on large issues. If we would give specific programmatic guidance by "costing out" alternatives, arbitrary delimination is essential and a rationale for such delimitation must be sought. Then one approaches the "local network" analysis, a minisystems perspective, of our later section, and which Burt and Blair introduce.

Sometimes in defining policy and often in specifying programming details, systems analysts employ tools of operations research. Operations research is constantly preoccupied with field tests of alternative approaches, in cost-benefit terms and from other perspectives; it is alert to "trade-offs"; it permits specific programming; it seeks feedback. It supports an effectiveness-efficiency policy and tends to be more consistent with centralization than with dispersed authority. It favors formalization.

Since there are now a considerable number of experiments with systems methods,[6] increased utilization in the future in planning

Table 4 Costs and Children Served in Four Short-Term Program Combinations[*]

Program	First Year[a] No. of Children	First Year[a] Cost ($000)	Second (and each later) Year No. of Children	Second (and each later) Year Cost ($000)
Alternative I				
24-Hour Screening	90–200	11	180–400	12
Emergency Caretaker Service	12–25	2	25–50	5
5 Emergency Foster Homes	36	9	73	18
30 Homemakers[b]	126	110	252	219
Reduction at Richland Village	162[c]	−26	325[d]	−75
TOTAL COST		106		179
Alternative II				
24-Hour Screening	90–200	11	180–400	12
Emergency Caretaker Service	12–25	2	25–50	5
13 Emergency Foster Homes	89	24	179	47
15 Homemakers[e]	73	55	146	110
Reduction at Richland Village	162[c]	−26	325[d]	−75
TOTAL COST		66		99
Alternative III				
24-Hour Screening	90–200	11	180–400	12
Emergency Caretaker Service	12–25	2	25–50	5
5 Emergency Foster Homes	36	9	73	18
4 Homemakers[f]	47	14	94	29
Reduction at Richland Village	83[g]	−17	167[h]	−51
TOTAL COST		19		13
Alternative IV				
24-Hour Screening	90	11	180	12
Emergency Caretaker Service	12–25	2	25–50	5
Reduction at Richland Village	18[i]	−1	37[i]	−1
TOTAL COST		12		16

[a]Based on 6 mos. program development time and only 6 mos. operating.

[b]24-hour, 7-day per week service.

[c]Amounts to 17 child-years (one child-year is equivalent to 365 days care for one child).

[d]Amounts to 34 child-years.

[e]24-hour, 7-day per week service.

[f]8-hour, 5-day per week service.

[g]Amounts to 10 child-years.

[h]Amounts to 20 child-years.

[i]Amounts to about one child-year.

[*]Reprinted by permission of The Urban Institute from *Options for Improving the Care of Neglected and Dependent Children* by Marvin R. Burt and Louis H. Blair.

Chart 1: Flow of Children Through Neglected and Dependent System, 1969

Reprinted by permission of The Urban Institute from *Options for Improving the Care of Neglected and Dependent Children* by Marvin R. Burt and Louis H. Blair.

social services is predictable. One recent study suggests the broader horizons that are opened. A *total* presentation of the blindness system, according to Donald A. Schon, involves:

that interrelated network of people, organizations, rules and activities which includes: (1) *all persons with severe visual impairments*; (2) *all agencies and groups that serve these people*; (3) *the training and research that affect these services*; (4) *the laws and policies under which services are provided.*[7]

Chart 2, dealing with one aspect of this, merely shows the resources expended in this system and their points of origin.

Any attempts to employ such models encounter lack of data, serious problems in setting widely acceptable boundaries, urgent need to curtail scope so as to make the approach manageable, and major political and administrative obstacles. Yet the analytic and practical advantages appear clear, if solutions are found; even if there is no political sanction, the analysis of a system yields valuable insights and important proposals.

Thus, at present, any broad planning effort in the social services should be expected to define a systems strategy on some appropriate level of generality and scope. Proponents of decentralization, community control, and participatory administration could find their activities in conflict with a systems emphasis. Legislators and executives will need to make choices. Advocates of other policy strategies with strong value justification but little empirical emphasis will also find themselves sharply questioned by systems analysts.

Market Strategies

The market model is familiar. It assumes that competition produces a better mousetrap, at a lower price. It is premised on the idea that the meeting of supply and demand in an arena in which consumers, producers, and middlemen are all seeking to maximize their own interests produces the best type of coordination and the most responsive system of production and distribution of goods and services. We have already seen how vouchers and performance contracting have been introduced into the social service field of late so that these advantages may follow. The evidence is not

Chart 2: National Resource Flows Related to Blindness

[1] This figure includes 118,130,000 of Veterans Administration funds which are allocated on the basis of visual impairment and are not limited to legal blindness.

[2] This category includes funds which could not be assigned with confidence to any other service category.

From Donald A. Schon, "The Blindness System," *The Public Interest*, 18 (Winter 1970).

yet in; preconditions essential to the strategy and possible dys-
functions have been cited (page 112).

The market model may be seen as an alternate model for service
planning. The "invisible hand" replaces the detailed design. Governmental agencies enact policies and broad programs. They vote
appropriations and set up guidelines. The profit or nonprofit groups
bid for contracts to deliver services. Or consumers are granted
categorical vouchers (for rent, food stamps, prosthetic devices,
tuition, transportation, and so on) for which private (and/or
public) agencies compete in the marketplace of services. In short,
the market strategy, when introduced to social service planning,
involves use of monetary incentives—rather than laws, policies,
and detailed program specifications alone—as the way to achieve
public objectives.[8]

Who would have predicted in 1960 that a society with increasing
social welfare commitments would, a decade later, be giving major
attention to market models? Bureaucratic insensitivity, a desire to
encourage service diversity, and a demand for more access by
ghetto populations to public resources, have joined to create this
new interest. The policy-conscious citizen will recognize, of
course, that market models need to be kept under control in the
social services. A market may reflect effective demand without
measuring need. Consumption rights should not be limited to what
the individual can command in the market, even if the market is
utilized as a service *delivery* mechanism. He will also note that
monopolies, vendor conspiracies, supply shortages, consumer
ignorance, if present, can make the social service market as unlike
the ideal type as the commercial market is often found to be. But
he probably will favor market approaches if he wants social services to be integrated into the economy with minimum impact on
the work ethic (a value choice) and if he wishes to avoid extensive development of centralized planning, large public systems of
service delivery, or service standardization throughout the country.

A market strategy in social welfare is defensible if so implemented as to either (a) enhance coordination or (b) promise the
kind of competition that will benefit the consumer. Always a
potential source of values contrary to the social welfare ethic
("access to service by nonmarket criteria"), market approaches
will need careful observation. Recently, in a brilliant comparative
study of methods of providing blood needed for transfusions under
different systems, Richard Titmuss has shown that altruism may

assure a higher quality product than do market incentives.[9] Using both economic and value criteria and contrasting the British system, which depends largely on volunteer donors, and the American, which depends significantly on paid donors, he shows that the nonmarket system produces a more reliable supply of blood for transfusions, with less waste and less administrative complexity, than does the market system. Moreover, American blood available for transfusions is of lower quality, more often carrying infection. Beyond this, however, in noting that freedom requires "breathing space" for altruism and in decrying the "Philistine resurrection of economic man in social policy," Titmuss argues against a totally utilitarian concept of the welfare state. He believes that altruism enriches society, in this sense, whereas market approaches may impoverish it.

The Local Network

A local network model is less grandiose than the full systems approach. It notes the complexity, when programming, of dealing with everything at once. A local network model, therefore, may deliberately ignore many dimensions that would be addressed by a full systems analysis of a field of service: most aspects of the relevant law, sanctions, finance, prevention, boundary maintenance, personnel administration, and so on. Sometimes the program planner or administrator who wishes to operate direct services efficiently, in a fashion consistent with a series of policy choices, and responsive to user needs, lacks sanction or facilities to "take on" all aspects of a field under any circumstances. More often delimitation is accepted in order to deliver services within a reasonable period of time. The limited local service network conceptualization is useful to such purposes. It is oriented to effectiveness and efficiency, but may be made compatible with decentralization and much employment of the voluntary sector.

A local network constitutes the service component of a system and the most immediate administrative supports for such a component. Requirements for such a network are identifiable.[10] The premise introducing a network model is that social services have a socially assigned task and are accountable to users and to the broader society. Whether conceived as universal or selective, such social services wish to deal with people considerately, respectfully, responsibly, and with equality. Whether public or voluntary, sectarian or nonsectarian, case services or utilities, therefore, they cannot be conceived as independent islands, as private principalities. It is appropriate to view them as responsible *for working in relation to one another* to accomplish socially defined tasks —and to be evaluated in relation to goal achievement.

What topics does this introduce to the planning agenda? What are a social service network's major dimensions, given such general policy?

Definition of Boundaries: One cannot organize an integrated service system without some agreement as to what will be encompassed. For the general social service planner this requires a decision as to whether mental health programs are part of the medical system or belong within its sphere. What of drug programs, services to the aged, programs for delinquents? Among the matters relevant to resolution of the boundaries issue are: what network boundaries will facilitate public understanding and use; what network boundaries will be efficient for the professions involved; what network boundaries are essential if the task is to be achieved, that is, if service efforts are not to be defeated by unmanageable fragmentation?[11]

The observer will note that boundary decisions involve policy. If general social services are administered along with income programs, relief recipients have a separate means-tested program (selectivity). If juvenile probation is handled within child welfare, there may be more emphasis on treatment than if it is separated (and stigmatized, perhaps) by a relationship to the correctional system.

Access Provision: Provision for access is a basic requirement for all service systems. Access machinery is especially important for the general social services insofar as they deal with people under stress and disadvantaged populations and adopt a rights concept. People do not categorize their lives or classify their needs in social service language or dimensions.[12] Universalism increases the urgency of access programs, but selective programs cannot forgo them. Citizens require *information* about rights, benefits, and services. When the information alone does not assure access, they may need more formal *referral*. If obstacles appear in their way, interfering with access to rights, they may require *legal assistance.* If the problem is abuse of administrative discretion or poor service, the need may be for *complaint machinery.* These access components are realizable in a variety of ways and in different relationships to one another, varying with both service and user characteristics. The quality of the access machinery determines whether general social services are "rights," whether they may have redistributional effect, and so on.

Assessment of Eligibility: Some public social utilities are available at user option, and there is no need, within the system, for any assessment of eligibility to draw upon it (some community centers, recreation programs, educational programs, and so on). Many other utilities are available by user status (over sixty-five, three to five, blind, physically handicapped, teenager, and so on). In most of such instances a simple registration procedure establishes eligibility. Services, if universal, may be free or may involve uniform user charges. Should there be differentiated fees, varying by income or family size or residence, more elaborate machinery must be set up.

In the instance of case services, the machinery must be even more extensive. Case services are assigned on the basis of illness, diagnosis, problem, need, and so on—that is, a category deemed as classifying people into groups whose members require a particular intervention. Such classification has traditionally been the responsibility of "intake machinery" in social agencies. Tests, examinations, interviews, observation, and other assessment devices may be used. Case services may also need to incorporate means tests, residence tests, and so on, as well, to allocate costs or control user populations—depending on the overall policy thrust.

For case services the eligibility assessment thus merges with the specification of the intervention, the "prescription." General social services are committed to individualized assignment of service components, as appropriate.

The assessment takes place at the doorway of the entire general social service network (if it is so organized) or at the doorway of individual agencies that may have their own "intakes" (Is this to be coordinated system or a marketplace?). In most systems, the general network doorway will be responsible for channeling, but the case service agency will need to do some case assessment to allocate the user to an appropriate service modality.

The utility, by contrast, will do much simpler classification—grouping in day care, selection of a compatible homemaker to visit an older person, introducing a teenager to a group in the local center.

Provision of an Interventive Repertoire: A network of utilities and case services is concerned with offering a range of resources, services, facilities, and benefits that will coincide with user needs and preferences, on the one hand, and the state of knowledge and professional skill, on the other. It is not a network if the repertoire is thin, outdated, offering few options and choices. Selective services will be less sensitive to this. Programs with little consumer participation will not enjoy the evaluative advantages of good feedback.

The implications of this requirement necessarily vary with the service category. It implies such notions as the following:

1. A child-care system that offers foster homes, large institutions, small group homes, agency apartments for adolescents, services for children at home, after-school centers, and so on
2. A training school system for adjudicated delinquents that offers many types of settings, among which are some offering general education, vocational training, psychiatric individualized treatment, group social psychological treatment approaches, differential security and degrees of integration of services with the local community, and so on
3. A program to help families in trouble that encompasses group education, casework, individual and group psychotherapy, supportive resources such as vacation facilities and homemakers, protective services, and so on

Case Integration: If social services are to be task-oriented—that is, are intended to enhance functioning or to solve personal problems, not merely to satisfy those who "give" or "do" services—a network must seek to maximize effectiveness through provision of case integration machinery. More specifically, devices are necessary to assure meshing of sequential and of concurrent case interventions into a situation. For example, if a child comes to the attention of the police, goes through juvenile court, spends time in an institution, and is helped by an after-care parole service while back at a public high school, a device is needed to assure that these several steps are additive, resulting in consistent help and a community responsiveness which strengthens conformity and adjustment. Similarly, if at a given moment a family is receiving service from a number of agencies, it is urgent that their efforts be mutually supportive. This is illustrated by the instance in which financial aid is being rendered by a public assistance department, a voluntary family agency is assisting the mother with a marital problem, the father is reporting regularly to a veterans administration mental health clinic, one child is of concern to a school social worker and another to an attendance officer. If the family is not seen as a "whole" and addressed (at the minimum) with a mutually consistent service strategy or (even better) by an overall approach consisting of mutually reinforcing components, little that is constructive can happen.

Program and Policy Coordination: This network component might have been listed first. The very notion of a network is premised on availability of specific instruments to assure the coordination of policy and program elements of the agencies that are part of the network. This does not mean that the network precludes competition, some inefficiency, diversity, or other devices that will keep it responsive and effective. The issue is how to guarantee that degree of coordination adequate to specified objectives, not perfect coordination and completely uniform policy. Enthusiastic advocates of the market would underplay coordination and encourage competition. They do not seek to construct networks.

Reporting and Evaluation: A range of instruments is needed to assess the output of the network as a whole and of its components and to propose improvements and departures:

1. Periodic large-scale evaluative research (measuring effectiveness)
2. Consumer feedback
3. Staff self-assessment
4. User boards or advisory committees
5. Experiments with alternative intervention repertoire components
6. Cost-effectiveness analysis

These reporting components are part of the accountability and public responsibility of socially established and supported community services. They are also important administrative, planning, and knowledge development tools. Without them, there is no network.

Should General Social Services Be "Freestanding"?

Should there be a distinctive general social services network at all? That initial decision has policy consequences not yet identified here. Like all policy issues, its referents are both in the world of facts and experience and in the world of values and preferences.

Sometimes a component of one social service subsector may be physically located in another. Thus, general social service outposts or core services may be based in schools or hospitals. An administrative issue of some importance, yet one on which there is little empirical evaluative evidence, is whether general social services should "stand free" in each community and constitute or be the hub of a network (that is, neighborhood counseling centers, family agencies, local authority social work departments as now being developed in Britain), or should the services be adjunctive to schools, hospitals, factories, settlement houses, social insurance offices, trade unions, and so on? In some instances acceptability and access would certainly be much enhanced by the latter pattern. The negative argument is that general social services placed within systems that have other primary missions may become the handmaidens of such institutions ("speed his return to work," "get him to behave in the classroom"), rather than focusing primarily on the client and his welfare, to the point of becoming his advocate. In other words, the organizational decision not to "stand free" could support a questionable policy. To which there are those who respond that socialization and promotion of adjustment, widely considered as humanistic goals, actually are the real constraints upon enhancement objectives in *any* social system.

The argument recalls the "investment" or "consumption" policy options for social services posed in an earlier section: Are the services valued per se or to advance other goals? In a society that is not monolithic in its objectives, in which people's perceptions of services cover a considerable range, and in which service rights as defined by law and collective bargaining are becoming important components of personal property, there probably will be a mixed solution to the issue. Some general social services will be "freestanding" and some will be adjunctive. Citizens will have choices. The important goal, however, if efficiency is valued, is the assured interrelations of network components, no matter where located. Social services that stand free should be connected with those integrated into other systems. Here, one of Cumming's conclusions is of special interest. Having discovered in her study of a city's social services network the considerable dependence upon and values of cooperative relationships based on informal consensus, she nonetheless argues on balance—as complexity increases —for a rational construction of a formal network ("formalization" is our term for the policy choice).*

Networks for Special Categories?

Social welfare legislation has tended to be categorical, since legislators and the executive branch respond both to interest-group pressures and public concern at a given moment with a specific problem. Therefore, there are programs for veterans, children, refugees, flood victims, the aged, the handicapped, drug users, and so on.[13]

Friends of categorical programs argue that they increase access. Veterans feel that they have a right to their own programs; old people know that certain programs exist for them. It is also argued that it is possible to obtain better public funding and to raise more voluntary funds for categorical problems than for general programs since the former tend to concentrate sentiments and to engender more interest-group activity. Finally, advocates of special services in this sense often hold that there are distinctive needs that are well served only by unique networks. In short, there are here questions for both policy maker and programmer.

Obviously, no matter how convincing the data about interrelations among needs and problems, no one can define an undifferentiated, accessible and efficient delivery system for the full variety of high-quality social services, broadly defined. Imagine *one* neighborhood service unit that is school, medical clinic, housing authority, employment agency, social insurance office, day center for the aged, and so on. The volume of need and the range of service is so great in all but the smallest communities as to create chaos if all is put into one operation. There can be one or more related buildings, perhaps, but several administrative bodies are

*Cumming distinguishes agencies on a continuum of "support" and "control" functions; interacting with a degree of professionalism are the diffuseness-specificity of service. She thus conceptualizes all social services as a control-support (regulative) system, with subsector boundaries not unlike (but not completely congruent with) ours. Elaine Cumming, *Systems of Social Regulation* (New York: Atherton, 1968). On the above point, see page 293.

needed. While appropriate linkages among such services are deemed vital, there is also general recognition that different programs enjoy varied public evaluations, are subject to differentiated professional dominance, and involve quite distinct patterns and delivery system requirements. Indeed, as previously noted, these factors have led to the separate growth and institutionalization of health, education, employment, income, and housing services. Where these separately institutionalized services employ social workers and related personnel, their tasks are seen as adjunctive.

However, even if the independently institutionalized human services or social sector services are eliminated and the focus is narrowed to what we have here defined as "general social services," the problem of designing a viable delivery scheme is still present! Is one unit to deliver probation, child guidance, school social work, family counseling, day-care services to the aged, home helpers, employment counseling, and services to several categories among the handicapped? Are there ways of packaging and interrelating services with more and with less likelihood of accessibility and effectiveness? Do some of the choices have favored or undesirable policy outcomes?

Social services experts have noted that it can be extremely harmful to those in need of case services to have the presence of a specific handicap deemed the critical basis for assignment of service responsibilities in all realms of a person's life.[14]

The crippled, blind, palsied, defective, and so on, have needs for medical care and rehabilitation services specific to their maladies and handicaps. But they also need housing, education, recreation, and work opportunity. There is some evidence that, if segregated by handicap for these other purposes, handicapped people tend to maximize what psychologists call "secondary gain." The handicap becomes the dominant life element and community integration is more difficult. This issue of service integration vs. segregation by handicap, only recently recognized, has wide ramifications. The Joint Commission on Mental Illness and Health called for a complete restructuring of services to the psychiatrically ill when it came to realize that their "casting out" from community life and segregation in isolated hospitals reinforced the illness. Several scholars documented a similar process among blind people, with resultant new emphasis on integration of the blind in "normal" institutional systems.

Special age groups (aged), problem categories (blind), and status groups (veterans) may need specialists or special services at some point. Nonetheless, wise policy would begin programming strategies on the assumption of a maximum role for the general social service system and an interpretation of that system as organized around service integration, rather than segregation. This would not preclude construction of a system that could tap specializations when and as needed, constantly coming back to and referring to the generalists who constitute the spine of the general social service network at the local level.[15]

Some exceptions will be necessary for administrative purposes or because of public preference and pressure. One would find it difficult to convince veteran lobbies that the policy of minimizing special services is wise, for example. Nor can the separativeness of correctional programs be wiped out very readily, even though the clientele of courts, police systems, and other correctional programs share many or most of their needs with those who come to general social services from nonauthoritative channels. Wherever possible (that is, whenever it is not absolutely essential that the public intervention involve the actual or potential deprivation of freedom) it is desirable to refer people out of correctional services into the general social services. However, since the degree of control and the exercise of public authority in some interventions must be considerable, the introduction of protections for due process is inevitable. A separate correctional system, albeit a reformed one, must remain. Recent Supreme Court decisions tend to make juvenile courts more, rather than less, like criminal courts, as formal protections are introduced.

Social service systems for migrants or a rural welfare system may be separately recognized in some places as solving specific problems of access and adaptability to clientele, but belong to and require integration with other general social services. Child welfare programs, services to the aging, physical and social rehabilitation are all well developed, but their separation out from general social services destroys the network and promotes dysfunctional fragmentation. The same may be said about counseling services for adolescents; such public social utilities as homemakers, home help, day care, meals-on-wheels; group treatment facilities of many kinds; a diversity of community centers; and general public multipurpose cultural and socialization resources.

NOTES

1. For example, see Alfred J. Kahn, *Planning Community Services for Children in Trouble* (New York: Columbia University Press, 1963); Eileen Younghusband, et al., *Living With Handicap* (London: The National Bureau for Co-operation in Child Care, 1970); Catherine King, *Preventive Child Welfare: The Feasibility of Early Intervention* (Melbourne, Australia: Melbourne University Department of Social Services, 1971).
2. For example, see Roland N. McKean, *Efficiency in Government Through Systems Analysis* (New York: Wiley, 1958); Robert Boguslaw, *The New Utopians* (Englewood Cliffs, N.J.: Prentice-Hall, 1965); Anthony Downs, "The Coming Revolution in City Planning," in Edward C. Banfield (ed.), *Urban Government: A Reader in Administration and Politics,* rev. ed. (New York: Free Press, 1969), pp. 596–610; and esp. Alice Rivlin, *Systematic Thinking for Social Action* (Washington, D.C.: The Brookings Institution, 1971).
3. Boguslaw and Downs are the bases for these summary sentences.
4. Rivlin, *Systematic Thinking for Social Action.*
5. Marvin R. Burt and Louis H. Blair, *Options for Improving the Care of Neglected and Dependent Children* (Washington, D.C.: The Urban Institute, 1971), pp. 7, 33.
6. For a recent public welfare attempt, see Jack C. Bloedorn, et al., *Designing Social Service Systems* (Chicago: American Public Welfare Association, 1970).
7. Donald A. Schon, "The Blindness System," *The Public Interest,* 18 (Winter 1970), 24–25; or see Robert A. Scott, *The Making of Blind Men* (New York: Russell Sage Foundation, 1969).
8. For the rationale, Anthony Pascal (ed.), *Thinking About Cities* (Belmont, Calif.: Dickenson Publishing Co., 1970), 82–90.
9. Richard M. Titmuss, *The Gift Relationship* (New York: Pantheon, 1970).
10. Alfred J. Kahn, "The Service Network as Heuristic and as Fact," in William Ryan (ed.), *Distress in the City* (Cleveland: The Press of Case Western Reserve University, 1969), pp. 163–172.

    Network studies, employing different network dimensions, may be illustrated by Elaine Cumming, *Systems of Social Regulations* (New York: Atherton, 1968); D. V. Donnison, *Welfare Services in a Canadian Community* (Toronto: University of Toronto Press, 1958); Margot Jefferys, *An Anatomy of Social Welfare Services* (London: Michael Joseph, 1965); Margaret Purvine and William Ryan, "In and Out of a Child Welfare Network," *Child Welfare,* 48, 3 (March 1969), 126–135; and Jean Packman, *Child Care: Needs and Numbers* (London: Allen and Unwin, 1968).
11. For a more formal discussion, see Alfred J. Kahn, *Theory and Prac-*

tice of Social Planning (New York: Russell Sage Foundation, 1969), Chapter 5; or Kahn, "The Service Network . . .".

12. Linda Winiecke, "Self-Determination of Need for Social Services Among OAA Recipients," *Welfare in Review,* July–August, 1971.

13. For illustration, see *Encyclopedia of Social Work, Sixteenth Issue,* 2 vols. (New York: National Association of Social Workers, 1971).

14. Eileen Younghusband, et al., *Living with Handicap.*

15. Ibid. This is the strategy of the United Kingdom's new local-authority social service departments.

Practice
Enacts Policy

If models reflect and affect policy, specific programming decisions are even more critical in this regard. This chapter offers illustrations of how the administrator or programmer utilizes program specification to advance goals—and of how less deliberate approaches to programming may defeat fundamental objectives.

To keep the presentation in reasonable focus and related to current social service realities, all of the illustrations are kept in the frame of a network approach to general social services at the local level, as specified in the previous chapter.

Access as Service

Access services are part of general social services. They are essential to such other social services as medical care, employment, housing, and social insurance—as well as to the more specialized and ongoing general social services. As noted earlier, access services include:

1. Information, advice, referral
2. Case advocacy
3. Class advocacy
4. Legal services
5. Complaint machinery

A so-called service network without provision for entry and channeling would obviously not deserve the designation, nor could it function effectively. Yet—for lack of adequate conceptualization and organization—many of the social services leave access to happenstance. The consequences have been documented in a library of studies and tracts; they affect both universal and selective programs:

1. Many agencies keep their caseloads to manageable proportions by avoiding publicity and serving only those who reach them through word of mouth or other limited devices.
2. Since access requires mobility, information, and initiative, some agency services are reserved for the more fortunate or "competent" among potential clients.
3. For lack of efficient channeling mechanisms, many people who need help suffer considerable buffeting until they reach a proper source of help, if indeed they ever do.
4. Many citizens never learn about rights, benefits, or entitlements that would ease their lives, enhance their routines, or enrich the development of their children—benefits ranging from social insurance, to educational programs, to vacation resources.
5. Consumers may fail to find adequate means of redress when mistreated, discriminated against, or closed out unjustly by administrative agencies controlling important services, by landlords, or by unscrupulous merchants or salesmen.
6. For lack of a place to turn in a personal emergency, especially a generalized emergency not clearly requiring firefighters, police, or an ambulance, many people suffer irreparable consequences.

These are consumer-related consequences, the most important of all to a social services system that considers itself humane and whose very raison d'être is the meeting of urgent personal, group, or communal need.

From the point of view of agencies and of the public at large, additional consequences must be mentioned:

1. For lack of adequate access machinery and channeling provision, social services involve tremendous wastage. People in need of advice or service go from place to place, sometimes never getting to the right place, sometimes getting to the right place after inordinate expenditure of "steering time" by personnel in a series of agencies, sometimes getting good service but misusing personnel where more "parsimonious" provision is possible.*

2. Since people in need of services will seek them wherever possible, a social services system without adequate channeling provision tends to provide biased access. Each agency to which a person comes by chance or recommendation to ask for help has a stake in the outcome. Some want more cases; some do not want any; some want particular types of cases. More formal access machinery, while not free of stereotypes and subject to the perceptual and prescriptive biases of the system it serves, is less likely to be tied to the stakes and limited perspectives of given agencies, their characteristic vantage points, and the unique assessment about the superiority of their service modes—which are normal for agencies.

In sum, whether one is concerned with making the system work more humanely and effectively for the user, or more efficiently and parsimoniously in view of communal stakes, a service network requires well-planned and appropriate access machinery. A policy of charity, focused on donors—rather than recipients—and not committed to efficiency, can ignore access. A "participation" strategy that favors encouraging people to "get theirs" by self-organization and confrontation will not want to regularize access,

---

*Under the principle of parsimony in treatment, the following obtain:
  1. The least disruptive intervention is the first treatment of choice.
  2. The least separation from family and job will be sought.
  3. The least expensive treatment will be used first.
  4. The least extensive treatment will be used first.
  5. The least trained intervenors will be used first.
"This means that most people will be cared for in their homes or job settings. Most will be cared for by caretakers and frontline agencies, except for acute emergencies. It means clinical personnel will be more involved in diagnosis and supportive consultation and training. It also implies that we will be using time trials of minimum, low-key interventions first, then picking up failures for more expensive and intensive forms of care." See William G. Hollister and Quentin Rae-Grant, "The Principles of Parsimony in Mental Health Center Operations," as abstracted in *American Journal of Orthopsychiatry*, 40, 2 (March 1970), 277.

since assisting people to find services and benefits has been
found to facilitate organization (as in the welfare rights movement of the late 1960s). Proponents of market strategies may not
wish to have standard routes into service systems, since this may
constrain competition.

Where access machinery is to be developed as congruent with
a network's philosophy and mission, it must command personnel
whose commitment is to the effectiveness of case channeling into
and within the network and whose professional discipline leaves
them unbiased as to the direction of channeling: all services
should have equal chances of receiving referrals, the determinant
being the client's situation and needs, professional knowledge,
and community policy.

Policy Questions for Access Services

A decision for universal services and to encourage and facilitate
utilization—rather than to shame users and hide resources (the
poor-law strategy)—calls for a general-purpose entry point to the
network as well as for information and referral competence at the
doorways of many organizations and institutions to which citizens
might turn. The universalism policy, oriented to seeing user as
citizen, focuses on efficiency and effectiveness in organization of
the network, since it assumes the right to information and to
service.

An attractive way to achieve the desired imagery and other
qualities, but not at all offered as the only way, is through establishment of what I would call a *neighborhood information center*.
The term is here employed for the entry point to the total social
services system, whether education, housing, public assistance,
recreation, social insurance, consumer guidance, homemakers, or
many other specific fields. The center would have to be a general,
unbiased, easily accessible, visible, unstigmatized, universally
usable facility. Its basic function would be information, advice, and
referral. If it could be set up so as to lead to public social utilities as well as case services, universal services as well as selective services, public services as well as voluntary, fee-charging
agencies as well as free ones, sectarian programs as well as nonsectarian, agencies involving more or less authority and control,
agencies suggesting client capacity as well as problem, the infor-

mation center would be truly accessible to citizens and would affect their access to services.

While there are circumstances under which such information centers could not be decentralized or need not be (sparsely settled countryside, rich suburbia in which all potential users can drive to a shopping center or a town center, areas of low-volume demand), under normal circumstances accessibility would be enhanced by decentralization to the immediate neighborhood: "within pram-pushing distance" or "where people get off the bus and shop" or "the most accessible point in every natural community of 50,000 to 100,000" or "in or near the post office or public library." Depending on local factors and the imagery sought, information centers might be freestanding or based in town halls, libraries, shopping centers, settlement houses, or other locations.

If the goal is to serve people, not to regiment them, a center, of course, is a *resource,* not a *requirement* when seen from the citizen's perspective. He is and must remain free to avoid channels and to go directly to any agency or program that seems right to him, and that agency must be equipped for considerate response, service, or referral. Anything less converts the network into a constraint upon freedom.

Neighborhood information centers and their equivalents would not eliminate the need for adequate doorway services—information, screening, and steering—in all agencies to which many people come of choice or necessity. The latter category would include health services, income maintenance programs, police stations, and libraries. Nor would such universal information centers preclude the development of specialized centers that have "natural" constituencies, centers whose existence would improve access for specific groups. The targets of more specialized centers might be conceptualized along several dimensions, the classification's validity and the center's specificity varying with time and place. Such centers, for example, might include those specializing in assuring access for old people, young drug users, veterans. Because certain groups and geographic areas face particularly difficult access problems, there has also been a tendency in recent years to make information, advice, referral, and case advocacy a major component of multiservice neighborhood centers.

The creation of access agencies (information centers or "hot lines") or access functions (doorway services in many agencies) does not, of course, relieve any given service organization of the responsibility to enhance the accessibility of its own specialized offerings. This may involve considerations and activities as diverse as publicity, public education, office location, office furnishings, provision of child-care arrangements for mothers who bring children with them, office hours, and the training of doorway personnel.

Even the specialized neighborhood information center might take one of several forms. Local social service programmers will find it necesssary, within this framework, to make locally appropriate policy and administrative decisions about the specific delimitation of functions for each neighborhood information center. This, too, represents a protection for diversity and freedom. Each choice involves a price, the sharpening of public image and agency response, community feeling about the service, client view of himself. Each possibility has validity, but all are not compatible, and local choices are inevitable.

We have noted elsewhere, for example, that some elements are basic in any information and referral office, whereas some are optional—varying with resources, other community provision, policy thrust, and the readiness to accept a given public image. This imagery, in turn, apparently affects who comes to the service and how agencies upon which the service calls respond to it.[1]

Essential Elements in a Neighborhood Information Center Program

1. To provide simple information, such as where something is located or how to get there
2. To provide information about more complex matters, such as the provisions of a law or an agency's function
3. To clarify the significance of a statute or of provision for a specific person (one aspect of the advice function)
4. To give advice on how to proceed—not only clarifying the possible, but suggesting a course of action
5. To steer the inquirer to an agency or service able to help, merely telling him what and where the service is, but doing nothing to help him get there
6. To refer to the right agency, going beyond steering to arrange for an appointment, send a referral letter or summary, facilitating the transition from inquiry to service
7. To provide a supporting, friendly relationship for those people whose continued welfare requires an occasional dropping in for

a friendly chat, often supplemented by information and advice
8. To help the inquirer with the contact—or to make it for him. (Sometimes the inquirer is helped to make the contact with a telephone referral or a letter. At other times the action required involves a letter of inquiry from the information service itself or an attempt to achieve a solution by mail.)

Optional Elements in a Neighborhood Information Center Program

1. To go beyond the presenting problem in helping people. (In general, social work services stress the need to see beyond the presenting request and to offer information, advice, referral, or help related to the real problem.)
2. To carry out formal diagnostic study
3. To carry out continuing counseling and treatment
4. To follow through (aggressively if necessary) until the inquirer has his needs or his rights recognized (case-oriented advocacy)
5. To seek program and policy changes in agencies (class advocacy)
6. To conduct general community education, where inquiries reveal widespread need for information
7. To recruit potential clients (outreach)
8. To monitor and report one's experience with human need and public provision. (A well-functioning information and advice service is, indeed, a window on the man in the street.)
9. To facilitate the self-organization of people with common problems. (The intent may be sociotherapeutic, group education, institutional change, or political action.)

The packaging of elements for the program of a given access service will derive partly from an estimate of the capacities of other local services already operating and partly from an estimate of the user population and the help it needs (are most of the people who will want service basically self-steering, able to use information, or are they people who need sustained support?). But it will also reflect the planners' sense of the local culture and the need to protect privacy, demonstrate "outreach" and concern, involve users as volunteers or policy makers for the center, employ the access service as a vehicle for service reform or expansion, and initiate social action.

Each decision along these lines involves a "price." Diagnostic "acuity" in the information service may frighten away potential users who want requests taken literally. A lack of outreach may signify "no interest" to other potential users. One must set priorities among potential local service consumers. One must estimate the burden of community need in making such decisions or, perhaps even better, find ways for potential consumers to help shape the definitions (another possible choice).

The definition of function thus carries wide implications. This is illustrated even more sharply with reference to whether an information center should carry out case and class advocacy or how such activities are to be provided otherwise in a network that assumes that social service access is a right that may sometimes need defending.

Case and Class Advocacy in the Access System

Case advocacy is an essential component in dealing with particularly deprived people who cannot themselves manage to cope with service networks, even if given information and steering. As defined in the above listing, it is quite compatible with an information-advice-referral service. Information center staff need to be equipped to know whether their suggestions work out and their referrals "take." If not, there must be provision for persistent follow-through with the service and follow-up with the client so that rights are implemented and needs met. A substantial literature on philosophy, technique, and ethics of advocacy of this kind is developing among helping personnel, particularly in social work.[2]

Sometimes community circumstances and agency structures may result in removing case advocacy from the neighborhood information center and placing it in other case services, such as counseling agencies. Sometimes the function is discharged in both settings. The issue is which agency has the capacity and freedom for persistent follow-through, the more competent and responsible staff, and a community image that will bring in the clientele needing the service. And which agency will be able to absorb advocacy without changing in an undesirable way or giving up entirely other essential functions?

The location and implementation of another essential function, class (policy) advocacy, poses an even more difficult and controversial question. At times an information center, multiservice center, or specialized agency learns that its referrals never "take." The service that should be available, the benefit that should be paid, does not materialize or is inadequate to its purpose. When this happens, some combination of the following is required: changes in laws, revised budgets, new procedures or adjustments in their application to the circumstances of some categories of individuals, reassignment of personnel, and so on. Under these conditions, case advocacy may help a given person, sometimes. Or it may be blocked by policy and provision. In either case, class advocacy promises larger payoff. Its techniques range from court challenges to laws and practices, to petition writing and traditional efforts to meet with responsible officials and to "negotiate" changes in policy and provision, to the more recent forms of "confrontation."

Obviously, this is one field in which choices must be made deliberately. Some class advocacy focuses on policy, some on program; some is oriented largely to aiding its immediate clientele, some to larger social objectives. Therefore, such advocacy sometimes considers it legitimate and appropriate to recruit clients to serve broader objectives than the solution of such clients' immediate "case" needs. How one (or how an organization) regards this depends on the decisions made about goal priorities. Such issues of function and priority are not easily ignored in the structuring of neighborhood information centers (or, for that matter, multiservice centers or any other social services that are oriented to redressing inequality, unfairness, and lack of access as experienced by minority and other deprived consumers).

Where class advocacy is not encompassed within the program of the neighborhood information center or multiservice center, it is generally assigned to either or both of two interrelated outlets: a community organization agency that undertakes social action and class advocacy (sometimes as a program component of a multiservice center or local antipoverty agency) and a legal services agency.

Legal services, thus, are an important element in the community access system. In the past, when privately funded, such services pursued class actions in a few major policy fields (for example, the work of the NAACP on segregation). Individual situations were not served per se, except where individuals could afford their own lawyers. Legal aid and similar services were employed largely to help poor defendants in criminal cases.

Since the advent of neighborhood legal services under the U.S. antipoverty program, which, in turn, inspired a number of related efforts, legal services have been available to poor individuals on a variety of civil matters, ranging from matrimonial actions to utilization of administrative appeals machinery and court process in relation to public assistance, housing, school suspensions, and so on. The result has been both a considerable strengthening of case advocacy and an expansion of class advocacy. Inevitably, major victories in court or before public boards are translatable into new rights for many additional clients. To illustrate we cite decisions in public welfare on residence laws and "man in the house" rules, or juvenile court decisions related to due process and proof. More recently new "law" has been made with reference to the "right to treatment" for institutionalized patients.

Middle- and upper-class individuals are able, themselves, to afford and to introduce legal talent where case and class actions are sought. For the poor, it is now widely affirmed, there should be available free or income-scaled neighborhood legal services. Some major programs in community action and consumer protection employ staff counsel in such roles. Experience with British Citizens' Advice Bureaus and U.S. local social services suggests that while neighborhood information centers can and must refer to neighborhood legal services, and while both are absolutely essential to the implementation of access, a strong case can be made for the separation of the two (although there are differences of opinion about this). They involve different professional disciplines, different public imagery and acceptance, and different responsiveness by service agencies that are their objects. A complete merger of information and advocacy may not in most contexts provide maximum access.

In sum, Cumming's[3] finding for Syracuse may be generalized: the differential flow of clients to various services probably reflects agency characteristics and the social system more than it does client troubles. Nonetheless, there is a movement from "gatekeepers"—people regulating access—to support and control services. Agencies tend to be either professionals' agencies (screening to produce a population suitable for the treatment in which the agency specializes and wishes to specialize) or clients' agencies (responsive to client troubles). An effective access system may rationalize the client flow if such is the community policy, may serve to increase agency responsiveness to client needs or lead to the creation of more services responsive to client troubles, and may even promote planning and more efficient employment of scarce resources. All of this is more likely to occur if the general policy is one of universalism and if the social service system includes a reasonable range of both public social utilities and case services.

None of this solves the service quantity problem in the many jurisdictions in which social services are in short supply. However, it does make it more difficult for agencies to solve shortages by making access difficult; it may improve the estimates of need; and it avoids solution of shortages by reserving services for those personally capable of achieving access without help. To summarize, the access function in a social service network is a critical factor in institutionalizing rights.

Decisions About Case Integration

Here we introduce briefly another general social service network task, case integration, to suggest other policy issues facing planners and programmers. The various professional role aspects of the topic are not explored.

Complex human problems and the multiplicity of needs in an urban-industrial society demand a multiplicity of specialized, or at least separated, social services. Where individuals or families are in considerable difficulty, help to them inevitably involves the mutual reinforcement and additive effects of services from a number of agencies and programs. Some of these services must be smoothly meshed in a sequential order lest the intervention effects at any given stage be wiped out: from acute hospital for the mentally ill, to the longer-term hospital, to community day group, to individual aftercare help, and so on. Some of the services are simultaneous, and their meshing is essential if they are to be mutually supportive rather than cancel one another out: the father's attendance at the veterans' psychiatric clinic, the family contacts with the public assistance worker, the mother-child visits to the school social workers, and the older brother's supervision by a court probation officer.

The segmentation of the social services is in fact a reflection of legitimate specialization. In part, too, it reflects the diverse motives that created an undifferentiated and punitive "poor law" for those unable to cope without help with society's daily require-ments, and then allowed subgroups to be differentiated out from the mass as changing social evaluations and deepening knowledge invalidated the earlier moral judgments. Simultaneously with the latter process, competent—or at least charitable—help was speci-fied. Fragmentation of services is also, of course, a reflection of tendencies among both professions and bureaucratic organiza-tions to retain and strengthen their own identities and to protect themselves by developing unique and loyal constituencies.

There is utility and validity in program specialization, relating as it does to the protection and development of uniqueness and expertise. But there is also in it a reflection of needs and motives not necessarily or solely related to the promotion of service goals and meeting of needs. The result, known wherever social services exist, is a pattern of service fragmentation, gaps, and failure to interrelate simultaneous and sequential service efforts for opti-mum effect. Many service failures, much wastage, and consider-able client disillusionment grow out of these facts.

Thus, a service network must seek to provide for case integra-tion, defined here as the sequential and simultaneous meshing of interventions directed toward a given client or user (individual, couple, family, group). Case integration is distinguishable from, although obviously related to, program and policy coordination as between agencies or among groups of agencies. The former focuses on the consumer of services. The latter relates to policy, provision, procedure, and agency interrelationships in terms of general principles and overall planning.

How, then, is the case integration function to be discharged in the general social services network? To a small degree, the staff of the neighborhood information center may be concerned with such matters, referring people with complex needs to a variety of places and managing the interconnections. However, most people given referrals or information at an information center are able to man-age the next steps on their own: they use the information, apply for the social utility, and pursue the benefit. Those with larger and more complex problems or less personal capacity require more help.

The transition, then, is to the case service category—helping services that are individualized by diagnosis or case evaluation.

Here one must ask about possible provision for case integration. Social service programmers have been seeking structural provision for case accountability, a fixing of clear professional responsibility to serve or guide a client, even if in the process there is also need for a specialist's assistance. There is widespread interest in the suggestion that the core case service in the general social service field be a generalist social work service, which would have the same relationship to the more specialized social services as does the general medical practitioner (GP) to the remainder of medical practice.[4] People who need individualized help, as contrasted with social utilities, would come to or be referred to the general social work service—for which a suitable name does not now exist.

The prototype is the general medical practitioner, the family doctor (with full recognition that the continuance of this role in the United States required its definition as a specialty, guarded by an Academy of General Practice!). In the instance of the generalist social work service or personal social service center (an alternative name) the general practice would inevitably be team or group practice. Medicine, too, is moving in such a direction in the United States. The pattern is now being established in the United Kingdom.

Generalist practice has many problems in the several fields in which it exists, and these should not be ignored by those who see it as a key component in a social service program model. All-purpose generalists may be, or may be believed to be, too "spread out" for the expertise needed to inspire confidence and to be effective. The elaboration of the function and the unanswered professional questions may be thrust aside for present purposes, however.[5] Here we may focus on the question of how or where the generalist social work service shall be developed. Or does it now exist? Again, major policy decisions affect the programming strategy: public or voluntary, universal or selective, general or separatist, sectarian or nonsectarian, bureaucratized or locally determined. Thus, answers to the question of auspice and mechanism for a generalist social work service depend upon or become a policy-planning process in a given place at a given time.

On the assumption of a universal approach in which the basic accountability is public, even though voluntary and private agencies may be contracted with to implement public responsibility, and on the premise that the goal is an organizational (bureaucra-

tized) solution to an organizational problem (service fragmentation and lack of continuity because units are separate)—but
favoring maximum opportunity for local diversity or autonomy, one
might urge creation of a local generalist social work service in
one or several of the following, the first being the most feasible
from a legal, resource, or structural point of view:

1. Local public welfare departments, now often called local social
   service departments, as they shed their public assistance eligibility functions under new federal administrative and legislative
   directives (public welfare thus shifting from selectivity to universalism)[6]
2. Voluntary family agencies and settlement houses, under contract with public departments and held to specific performance
   requirements (For family agencies, this must involve a major
   shift in functions; for settlements that are multifunction agencies, it requires creating a subunit for the role; for both it must
   mean acceptance of more public guidance of "voluntarism.")
3. Local community action (antipoverty) service units or units
   created for the express purpose by antipoverty neighborhood
   corporations (This would require clear separation of social
   action and class advocacy from the service function, as well as
   more professionalism and a greater readiness to employ and
   utilize professional personnel than has characterized most such
   groups; but it would increase selectivity and community variability.)
4. Local Model Cities, community school, neighborhood renewal,
   or community mental health agencies (Each of these suffers
   major disabilities because in total the units do not add up to
   community coverage, have other primary missions, may not be
   able to attract all users needing the service because of existing imagery. But it integrates social services with other institutions—an investment perspective.)

Social service programmers committed to a generalist service
will in each instance wish to weigh the local advantages and problems of each option.

Storefronts and Multiservice Centers

The interplay of policy with administrative strategy (in this
instance the conception of the functional requirements of a local
social service network) are well illustrated in a discussion of

whether or how storefronts and multiservice centers should be planned as part of the network. Currently storefronts and multiservice centers enjoy popularity with the media, federal funding agencies, and the professional journals, all of which see them as essential components of decentralization of services.

The development of such facilities should be seen in the context of a widespread revolt against prevailing patterns of social service organization, as the failures of traditional patterns to facilitate access and assure delivery of services to all population elements and all parts of the city became apparent. Throughout the 1940s and the 1950s social service organizations had tended to centralize, and their delivery modes had been increasingly standardized. Now, in reaction, came a move that stressed diversity, local policy flexibility or control, indigenous staff, informality, easy access, one-stop service, a mixture of service receipt and one's own involvement in the rendering and changing of services. Storefronts and multiservice centers became major vehicles.

Storefronts and multiservice centers are and can be many things, and an assessment of their potential and desirability in a social service network must depend upon what they are designed to be and become in a given place at a specific time. There is danger, as Edward O'Donnell has noted, that such centers will become an "organizational Twiggy," temporarily capturing the public imagination and causing disregard of the merits of other useful models and long-term experience. On the other hand, storefronts and multiservice centers can be shaped to fill specific gaps and to play needed roles in a network in which other components are strengthened and utilized.[7]

The storefront's major merits are informality and locale. If the goal is to localize or decentralize (the former implying central control and the latter some decentralization of policy or programming authority), there is need for a comfortable and convenient outlet. Poverty areas and racial ghettos have many empty, visible, convenient stores. Neighborhood information centers, centers offering generalist social work services or specialized programs such as job placement are easily set up in such locations, because they require little more than desks, files, phones, typewriters, and simple partitions. Especially if indigenous personnel are to be employed, a storefront location may represent convenience and comfort.

There is, however, a negative argument that cannot be completely ignored—with the decision perhaps ultimately resting with local people. There are those who resent the dreary and shabby storefront, even if it is cleaned up, reasonably furnished, and supplied with a coffee urn and milk bar for the convenience of parents and children in the waiting room. Why, they ask, should facilities not be better than the level prevailing in the poverty area? Why poor surroundings for deprived people? Why not good buildings, more conventional offices, more privacy? There is obviously need for a trade-off and balancing point, reflecting prevailing preferences: familiarity vs. improvement, convenience vs. equality.

But *function* is more important than the type of housing for the office. Storefronts may be specialized or multipurpose, information centers or places to organize social action. They are part of the decentralization strategy. The decision to use or not use them is independent of planning with reference to multiservice centers, despite the constant joining of the two in discussion and analysis. The question remains: where *does* the multiservice center fit in relation to the series of functions that belong in the general social services network?

First, the multiservice center is often a place where several networks may meet for service delivery: visiting nursing, employment placement, family counseling, housing complaints, neighborhood legal services, or public assistance "intake." The center may play this role whether in a neighborhood storefront or a downtown office building, but the more recent linking of storefronts and multiservice centers is motivated by the conviction that a multiplicity of social services and other communal functions should be joined for one-stop convenience in the immediate neighborhood.

Its more expansive proponents see the multiservice center as a neighborhood base that combines information–advice–referral–case advocacy with decentralized service outlets for a variety of voluntary and public social services, meaning by the latter both general social services in our sense and services belonging to more specialized systems. The argument is that this kind of service organization increases access and facilitates case integration. (The latter is referred to generally as "coordination," but the function intended is case integration, in our sense.) Seldom identifying the general practice social service role per se, these proponents tend to see the information–advice–referral personnel (often local case aides) serving as "social service" or "urban" brokers and as case advocates, helping disadvantaged people (to use their language) "to negotiate the complex bureaucratic systems that deny them service." While not formalized or professionally specified, there is some implicit assumption that the broker is a case integrator. He is seen as offering expertise and advice about services, but not as a skilled personal counselor. For the latter type of help, one uses a family service agency, adult psychiatric clinic, and so on.

Conceptually, then, the multiservice center may be defined as an attempt to create a social services network in one location. It would be a complete one-stop social services "department store," a shopping center in which one has a guide (an "urban broker" or "case aide"). All the functions deemed essential are provided, and there is convenience of location—whether the poverty area storefront, the downtown office building, or the office space in a commercial shopping center complex. This ideal model is logical and attractive. Its rarity as an operating entity in the world of daily service operations must be seen as a caution sign for social service programmers: Are the limitations that are widely identifiable indigenous to the model or idiosyncratic to the local circumstance? One tends on the basis of available research, consultant reports, and observations to suspect the former; but the case is not closed.[8]

Multiservice centers are seldom equal to the promise implied in the name. For example, they generally do not provide for the critical generalist social work practitioner coverage, which is the anchor point for case services. This is no occasion for surprise: the general practice role is often relegated in multiservice centers to information and referral personnel, who are not equipped for ongoing counseling. Or the general practice task may be assigned to family service agency personnel, who are more specialized casework therapists and do not ordinarily assume the full general practitioner responsibility.

Nor would one wish information-referral services to carry the imagery of or to demand the professional qualifications and control for general social work practice. Most users of information-referral services are likely to be in need of facts about rights and entitlements (consumer rights, social security benefits, and so on), to be in need of referrals to or application forms for public social utilities (day care, homemakers, community centers, and so on), or to require services in other than general social service programs (housing, income maintenance, employment, and so on).

This would not preclude the sharing by information-referral services and others of building space or the joint participation in a multiservice center if circumstances permitted the projection of an image encouraging broad usage, even by people who did not consider themselves as having personal "problems."

Multiservice centers also have difficulty in becoming true local outlets for specialized services, such as job placement, housing application processing, well-baby clinics.* Any such effort confronts counterpressures quite familiar to students of organizational dynamics. A health department may agree to place a well-baby clinic in a multiservice center, but in fact soon finds that it cannot provide the necessary specialized equipment and personnel for several such centers, even though the pledge may be fulfilled for a major "demonstration" project. The usual substitute arrangement is a public health nurse, available at specified times each week, who renders simple services and channels most users to the health department or hospital clinics.

Employment and housing offices respond similarly: they either find that they cannot manage all the needed specialized personnel, or the complete duplication of job or housing files, or the coordination mechanisms that are indispensable if the same core services, utilizing the same resources, are delivered at two locations. The solution is usually the assignment of a "partial service" outpost—rendering what is simple service (usually referral and information) and routing the inquirer to the main office for the core service.

When this occurs, the multiservice center has become an information–advice–referral–case advocacy location whose services are strengthened by the presence of specialized liaison personnel from a number of agencies whose services are in high demand. The latter are to be seen as largely enhancing the information center function, however, their expertise and contacts presumably assuring more accurate advice and more potent referrals.

The obstacles to delivering an agency's full service through multiservice centers under shared administrative authority or under a new local auspice go well beyond the problem of setting up a complete service requiring specialized personnel and equip-

*O'Donnell documents the fact that relatively few public welfare offices place outposts in multiservice centers.

ment. One could invent solutions to such difficulties. Also operating is an organizational-political tendency that must be recognized. Agencies receive public support, staff, equipment, and authority as they become visible and develop consumer, staff, and political constituencies. Whether correctly assessing the importance of the phenomenon or not, most departments consider themselves better off if they have visible, local outlets that are clearly identifiable, employ significant numbers of people, and are valued by citizens. Therefore, when asked to sacrifice some of their visibility and to share a facility under *other* auspices, they are hesitant and may take half measures. Or, if their units remain in multiservice centers, they are often permitted to become independent enclaves.[9]

Nor do multiservice centers assure the program coordination and case integration that is always part of their rationale. Their doorway personnel undertake a measure of information–advice– referral–case advocacy. But, without a general practice unit or a tradition of general case accountability in any of their subunits, they do not typically offer the service to the average run of cases. The organization offering initial auspices and housing for the center tends to conceptualize the unit as enriching its own offerings and supplementing its own coverage (antipoverty, health, mental health, housing, employment), not as meeting all of the neighborhood's social service needs. Nor does the governing or administrative structure of such units allow for remedying the gap once it is acknowledged.[10]

Most multiservice centers seem to manage to implement a *few* fully specialized services, however, reflecting the center's auspices, special local needs, and unique motivations. A number may, for example, conduct youth training or employment programs. Some house very effective and complete neighborhood legal services. Others offer consumer counseling that is comprehensive and of high order. Many carry out child care and Head Start. When the job load becomes heavy, they act as does any agency: they become "legalistic" and find ways to limit their caseloads.

The typical multiservice center, then, is not really the comprehensive, one stop, department store of services that is often discussed. It is, rather, a conveniently located facility (which may be anything from a neighborhood storefront to an elaborate central building) that combines the access function with a limited number of specialized services from within the general social service system and from other social welfare components. It may also be structured to assure consumer involvement at a number of levels. But it does not comprise a complete network. In fact, it usually lacks a generalist social work service and provision for case integration.

All this is stated by way of description, not critique. Multiservice centers, set up as described, may be very useful. They currently suffer because the interdepartmental or interagency arrangements that must accompany their establishment do not ordinarily include sufficient surrender of sovereignty or guarantee of power to provide for an administrator or board capable on a day-to-day basis of weaving even the limited components into an operating network. For the most part their subunits report to different organizations and are supported and evaluated by different boards. They may have different views of clientele and their needs, and even independent agenda for the multiservice center. They offer locational convenience, not a network.

One could project some general improvement if multiservice centers were to be organized on the basis of more surrender of sovereignty. Antipoverty boards, Model Cities committees, and others who plan them often possess enough financial power to assure a greater measure of coordination and provision for case integration. Were they to do so, multiservice centers would make a larger contribution to the delivery of services. Experience compels skepticism about the likelihood of enough meshing of units and adaptation of role fully to realize the initial goals; at most the multiservice center may offer convenience and several components of a network. Such centers could become part of a planned network.

Some experiences with drug control programs, rehabilitation, and the retarded suggest another possibility: the multiservice center that offers all network elements related to one problem or group. Here the motivation, power, and conceptual clarity necessary for a network in one location may be brought together.

Thus, the multiservice center is probably, as O'Donnell states, a Twiggy—but it has its possibilities. A community needs a multiservice *network*, providing for all network functions, and multiservice centers can contribute to it.

We have yet to turn to the question of user participation in policy and service delivery in such centers or elsewhere within service networks, and to the related matter of the wedding of direct service with social protest and social action.

Direct Service and Social Action

To begin with the latter, the issue has an interesting recent history, although there have been earlier and in some ways similar developments in American social work at several points over the past one hundred years.

In the early and mid-1960s social workers and aides working in local antidelinquency and antipoverty neighborhood service centers,[11] imbued with an accountable ideology of "reaching out,"[12] pioneered in what we now refer to as case advocacy. Where agencies did not deliver the announced or legally prescribed services, these new-style workers followed through. Where clients could not themselves cope with the complexity of procedures and requirements standing between them and the help needed, the social workers or aides went along and assisted whenever necessary. Later, if it appeared that unfair agency practice, questionable rules, or arbitrary judgment deprived needy citizens, these social workers or aides teamed up with the new and emerging neighborhood legal services to challenge decisions before appeal boards and in the courts. Given the needs of the groups served and the program focus of the day, these actions tended to select for their targets public welfare departments, housing authorities, and school boards.

The action to this point, it should be noted, was oriented to serving the individual client. One went from application, to advocacy, to legal action because of the obstacles discovered en route.

The escalation from these measures to "class actions" in the legal sense, and to social action generally, was natural and probably inevitable. Follow-up with an agency, one case at a time, is time-consuming and frustrating. One might achieve some positive results for the given case, while knowing that there were hundreds of others like it. Why not change the policies or administrative practices affecting everybody? Why not amend the laws that bind the hands of agency personnel? Why not reform staff practices? Shared responses of this kind, affecting the dedicated staffs of these new programs, led to a buildup of "class action" cases through the legal services—cases that sought rulings affecting many people by showing procedures, requirements, and provision to be inequitable and unconstitutional.

At the same time, the various outlets for social action were pursued to obtain better legislation relating to public assistance, housing, health, and schools. Where the issue was not the statute but procedure, administration, professional practice, or budget levels, these became the targets. The methods eventually ranged from delegations to officials, petitions, letter writing, lobbying, to sit-ins, mass demonstrations, rent strikes, public confrontations, to office vandalism and destruction of facilities.[13]

We have described this as a development growing out of experience in case advocacy and commitment to serve people in need. In one sense, from the perspective of the direct-service practitioner, it was. In another sense there is a broader explanation: antidelinquency and antipoverty programs of the mid-1960s began with what are essentially *service* strategies, even though they carried out innovations within such strategies. Basically, their goal was to offer training, access, and motivation as a way to remove inequality that blocked opportunity. True, they placed less emphasis on personal treatment and guidance and more on job training and education than had earlier service programs; nonetheless, their object was the victim and his reform or retooling.[14] Slowly, a number of leaders in local community programs, their academic consultants, and even their governmental and foundation supporters, began to question such strategy, particularly as it affected the black population. Diagnosing the core problem as communal "powerlessness," they saw little likelihood that individual help could pay off (or even be well done) except in the context of institutional reform. And the latter was seen as requiring local mobilization of, and political action by, deprived neighborhood people. Here, too, there was a shift from initial interest in social action directed at improving schools, welfare departments, and housing authorities, among other institutions (class actions and policy advocacy) to a demand for either community control of or participation in control of such institutions. "Maximum feasible participation" had become the slogan. Clearly, the major vehicle was now social action merging into political action. If the former sees program change as its objective, the latter seeks political power. Case services become secondary.

We need not trace the evolution of the process through the late 1960s and early 1970s for present purposes. Poverty areas, ethnic and racial ghettos, Indian reservations, and even prisons have become politicized. Social action has escalated both in volume and in militancy. What is now to be confronted by the social services programmer is the organizational question of the relation of direct social services to case and class advocacy and to social action in a service network. The issue, we shall hold, is a real one, and must be faced even by the most sympathetic advocates of the entire process here described.

Although the evidence is limited and opinions vary, it appears that the client in need of service does better in a neighborhood information center, general social work service, specialized agency, or multiservice center dedicated to case service, up to the point of case advocacy and—perhaps—policy advocacy, but not undertaking the social action aimed at wider objectives as well. Where the one organizational entity assays both functions, people in need of direct service may be recruited for demonstrations and protests, or as class action "documentation," to the sacrifice of their personal needs.* Social action strategists, given their tasks, cannot avoid converting service needs into social action "ammunition." But to the programmer or administrator whose focus is on service, not on social action, such an approach represents unreasonable exploitation of people who enter an agency seeking immediate personal help. From this perspective, it is not inappropriate for a social action organization to utilize the circumstances, needs, and testimony of those who freely join it in order to attain its objectives, nor is it inappropriate for such an organization to go out to seek evidence and witnesses to advance its goals. What is questioned by those who would protect direct services is only the conversion of a request for personal help to what is publicly perceived as a direct-service agency into a recruitment device and use of the applicant, thus diverting or converting the appeal.

The joining of the direct-service task with the social action role within one organizational unit has another undesirable consequence—unless one's commitment is only to political action. Agencies to which neighborhood information centers or multiservice centers refer for benefits and specialized services have found it confusing to receive service requests from an organization at one moment and to be picketed by it at another. They have become suspicious when case developments are used against

---

*Systematic data are limited. The findings may be different for child advocacy programs, which combine case and class approaches focused on improved service delivery, than for other programs whose political goals are central. See Kahn, Kamerman, and McGowan, *Child Advocacy: A National Baseline Study.*

them in administrative hearings and in court actions. The result is that where social action, case and class advocacy, and direct service are combined, a kind of inevitable process operates: it becomes more and more difficult to obtain services for clients through other agencies if such agencies know that they may also be attacked for policy and practice by the referring group.

Grosser sums up as follows:

The separation of services and action functions into discrete organizations is suggested because the two functions are frequently in disharmony . . . and because the dispensers of public agency services are congenitally and organizationally unable to distinguish between the protest and service function when practiced by the same organizations.[15]

If the policy is to assure service availability, then, a local service network planner should probably not attempt to organize social action and social protest through the agencies that channel people into or that render direct services. Indeed, despite a continuing debate, most service agencies have apparently arrived at such a decision. However, service agencies as well as specialized units may be able to contain a measure of case and class advocacy.* Nor does a limitation on such development or on broader social action in service agencies necessarily signify a failure to recognize the need for consumers, clients, and citizens to organize in order to affect policy and programs. It may involve electing an alternative approach, the support for special outlets in the service network for this purpose (community assemblies, administrative boards, advisory committees, client organizations, neighborhood groups), or may signify conviction that the social policy and program concerns must be made more visible within the general political system. Social provision and social services are important enough to modern society to be at the center of public policy debate and advocacy.

"Participation" was listed in an earlier section as one of the proposed objectives of social services. Some multiservice centers organize clients for self-help that falls far short of social action and protest. Included are tutoring, cooperative child care, clean-up

---

*I am not yet prepared to generalize about the boundary between class (policy) advocacy and social action with broader goals than service system change or reform, if these are located in a non-service agency.

campaigns, giving "advice" to program people, implementing a new service. The goal is the strengthening of the individual participants and encouragement of local leadership. Such programs, basically sociotherapeutic, can be contained within direct service agencies without undermining the core function. They do not seem to thrive because deprived population groups find this kind of activity unfamiliar, based as it is essentially on a middle-class self-help ethic. Those who seek more aggressive social action define it as a diversion.

Consumers and the Control of Social Services

In the search for program responsiveness and "relevance" there is currently widespread interest in and support for considerable user-client-citizen involvement in the planning and assessment of social services. Historically, legislative bodies, public officials in the executive branch, and paid staff, in their development of policy, creation of programs, and delivery of services have often displayed shocking lack of sensitivity to the problems, priorities, and realities faced by disadvantaged community members. The latter high-rate utilizers of some services (public assistance, public general medical programs, public psychiatric facilities, courts, and police) often found themselves offered programs in which they were major "consumers" and the advertised "beneficiaries," but that were in no way attuned to their needs. The civil rights and antipoverty "revolution" of the 1960s and 1970s therefore included, along with its many other provisions and its stress on decentralization, some components designed to bring the traditionally disadvantaged consumer into a position to influence policy making, programming, and service delivery.

To the extent that they are identifiable as serving poverty areas and districts, or disadvantaged ethnic and racial groupings, therefore, neighborhood information centers, multiservice centers, and specialized public or voluntary programs, have introduced "members of the community" to position of influence as members of governing boards, policy committees, advisory committees and as service volunteers or paid, indigenous aides. Similar practice has been followed in local antipoverty community corporations, Model Cities corporations, and other comprehensive programs that operate or contract for a range of services. The scale is significant but

—according to the O'Donnell studies cited above—the practice is not nearly as prevalent as professional literature might seem to suggest. Although operational problems are many and conflict among competing local groups considerable, this trend to decentralize power and democratize the advisory, administrative, and policy functions is in the spirit of the social service network and its assigned mission in the sense of our discussion. It is consistent with the notion that human services must be responsive to users and subject to their reactions. We would expect individual agencies to be enriched and improved by the process, and there is anecdotal reporting that says that they are. Problems and obstacles are also visible, however, and obviously require attention if the full potential of consumer involvement is to be realized.

The two major identifiable issues may be formulated as follows:

1. What is the boundary between professional and consumer prerogatives in agency governance and administration?
2. How should those responsible legally resolve competing claims of citizens to represent "communities" served by agencies?

A number of the ultimate ramifications of these questions need not be here explored (see pp. 120–124). We take as point of departure the premise that there are some services that for reasons of substance or of history operate locally on the basis of policy developed at higher levels, often in statutes, and whose staffs are controlled within structures of bureaucratic organization. Local committees are, then, advisory and focus on program.* At the other extreme, there are some social services that allow very substantial local policy making, as well as programming. Here local bodies may become governing or administrative boards. Where such boards have statutorily defined rights with relation to significant aspects of budget, staffing, or administration, the phrase "community control" may be said to apply. In between are most agencies, allowing some local policy options and some local programming, and capable of sustaining a variety of degrees of consumer involvement, depending on how the power relationships emerge.

Here the two questions posed above appear salient. Professional

---

*O'Donnell found that public welfare clients were more often appointed to advisory committees than to policy-making boards. See Edward J. O'Donnell and Otto M. Reid, "Citizen Participation on Public Welfare Boards and Committees," *Welfare in Review*, September–October 1971.

practice is interlaced with value and preference components, with judgments as well as with scientific knowledge. If there is interest in that consumer involvement which does not undercut service quality, it will become urgent during the next several years to identify the realms in which members of the several professions must be permitted to render professional judgment and to make decisions for which they are accountable. It will also be urgent similarly to delineate when they may be subject to lay boards and their decisions. The difficulty of this question is best appreciated if one considers the types of choices inherent in curriculum development in elementary school, recreation programming in after-school centers, the operating of a residential treatment center, counseling approaches in a family agency, and the choice of substitute care arrangements for an abused child. Contrast the value components among such options with the expertise-value components in an engineer's decisions in planning a bridge or a surgeon's in deciding whether to operate. Because the social services rest on quite limited validated knowledge, have in many instances only vague notions as to their own effectiveness, and rely for implementation on non-, pre-, and paraprofessionals as well as on fully qualified and licensed practitioners, social services find it difficult to make a case against considerable consumer involvement even in the details of programming. Such involvement, while obviously desirable since these will always remain services in which value choices are central, must not be so defined and implemented as to discourage and inhibit knowledge development and strengthening of technique. Otherwise, there will be no basis for improvement in practice; there may even be a true decline in quality. The issue is urgent; the solution, long range.

The second question is essentially political: How is a decision to be made about who is the "community" to be represented on local administrative boards or policy or advisory groups? Even in minority communities and deprived areas one finds what Norton Long has called an "ecology of games."[16] In a bid for a voice in local institutions and services, or for what is locally referred to as "a piece of the action"—to express the notion that one is dealing with jobs, business, and power—neighborhood residents find themselves wooed by competing local racial, ethnic, and political groupings. Or the group identification and ideologies may be secondary to the personal rivalries of different aspirants for careers of leadership.

Particularly in the past half-decade, the results have often been irrational, wasteful, and of little apparent advantage from the point of view of services per se. The positives, too, are readily identified in the sense that new political leadership has emerged, had valuable training, and developed a base for action, while previously discounted segments of the population have made themselves heard or obtained jobs and contracts. In effect, the political issue has had to be settled and the service question has inevitably been secondary. In an effort to open new doors, bring forth new leaders, and redress long-term wrongs, the issue of "who is the community" has often been answered in terms of balance of power in local confrontations, visibility, following, persistence, and similar political criteria. Increasingly and (we would hold) properly, however, the matter is being referred to the political process. Democratic societies, for all their failings, have some experience with the periodic use of the ballot box to choose leaders and to seek the consent of the governed. Where the right to speak for a community is in contention, a society can do no better than appeal to elections and seek to assure widespread participation in the voting (local, decentralized school boards and Model City boards). Or elected officials may be called upon to designate appointees and to bear the consequences if local citizens consider them to be unrepresentative. Neither process precludes a degree of ethnic or racial or class preference at a given time and place, to redress long-term wrongs and bring new voices to the table. Political leaders can and should "risk" such designation. For some purposes a given proportion of places on committees might be reserved for experienced "users" (welfare mothers, day-care parents, public housing tenants, parents of retarded children). Where such users do not, alone, express the total public interest, they should not be regarded as the sole community spokesmen.

Consumers, in short, can and should be seen and heard in the various roles relating to the planning and administration of social services. Given contention as to who the representatives of such consumers are to be, elective and appointive procedures can be developed that are democratic and rational.

We may expect yet another type of consumer involvement should the use of categorical vouchers (see page 112) expand. For one thing, consumers with money or vouchers to pay for service may "vote" with their feet. Their "control" takes the form of avoiding poor service. Also, given current interest both in consumer cooperatives and in local antipoverty development corporations, it would be quite feasible for people with access to categorical vouchers for day care or housing or nursing service to pool their entitlements, create a board of directors, and establish new service agencies under their own control.

Thus far the discussion has concentrated on closed-out citizens, the poor and other disadvantaged minorities, and their involvement in the governance of social services. But our overall thesis is that all social service requires renewal, that the post-industrial society must update its public social utilities and invent many new types of provision. There is therefore a case for a policy of consumer involvement of the several sorts in all kinds of services, whether or not decentralized, whether or not of special importance to the disadvantaged. New vehicles for such involvement, new rights for consumers, and new channels for participation are required wherever social services are rendered.

Renewal

While not the only possible policy, one widely held view—which has been our premise in much of the discussion—is that the purpose of a social services network is the rendering of service. Social control is a by-product. Individual and community protection are secondary tasks. In this sense, then, ultimate judgments about a network's worth should refer to quantity, quality, significance, and accessibility of both concrete and practical facilities and resources, as well as less visible but much needed personal guidance and counseling to help those in trouble in their coping with growth, relationships, and crises. The range thus includes child-care arrangements, home helps, provision of furniture and food stamps, vacation facilities, prosthetic devices, telephones for isolated old people, scholarships to cultivate a child's special talents, and train tickets—as well as tutoring, advice, information, counseling, psychotherapy, socialization experiences, group activities, foster homes, adoptive parents, and so on.

Social agencies, like all organizations, are in constant danger of confusing supportive and maintenance activities related to the welfare of the organization with the rendering of the core service. Good access services and adequate provision for coordination and case integration are worthless unless the end product is a needed service, competently delivered, at the appropriate time. And we must also stop periodically to recall that, if social services are to carry the functions of acculturation-socialization-development, access, and help-therapy the specific services designed to implement such functions must be updated from time to time. Moreover, as social policy shifts, the balance between and among such services is in need of constant review and adjustment.

The U.S. social welfare scene underwent a shift in its focus in the 1960s from therapy, guidance, and probation to education, job counseling and training, placement, and role training as prerequisite to the "opening of opportunities" to those previously closed out by major social institutions. Later, income maintenance and political participation took the center of the stage.[17] Conceptually, this was a shift from emphasizing the use of social services to facilitate adjustment and conformity, and to strengthen motivation, to a view of services as opening opportunity, as mobilizing human resources. Then services became a vehicle for monetary and "power" redistribution. Yet, despite the shifts in preoccupations of new programs, only the unperceptive, who believed that all poverty was "one lump" and all social problems the product of one cause, could argue for the closing out of guidance, counseling, personal help, foster care—and other "older" programs.[18]

Those who would plan and implement social services, whether in a given, local agency—or from an administrative base that influences a total network—must ask, then, whether the balance is correct, for their time and its policy thrusts, as between concrete, "hard" services and the guidance-relationship types of help, between access facilitation services and services expecting changes in the individual, between mobilizing people and changing them, between services premised on utilizing peoples' talents and characteristics and services focused on developing capacities and socializing into new patterns, and between services viewing users as patients and those which see them as clients. To concern oneself with correctness of the balance among optional modes is to understand that the matter is not one of "either-or" in a social services network with several functions. It is also to imply that within each of the service types there is updating to reflect knowledge, skill, user wishes, user characteristics, and institutional change.

Just as social service systems have found it difficult to change in response to need for new balance among service types, so has there been difficulty in updating of methods. For, if the thesis is correct that modern urban industrial society has not yet learned to cope institutionally with the social change it has generated, then the need for social invention is considerable. If the argument is valid that among the responses should be a considerable expansion of public social utilities and a much improved pattern of case services—then the challenge for social service planners, programmers, and practitioners is clear. Somehow, there must be assembled in the major areas of need enough professional competence, knowledge, resources, organizational flexibility, user involvement and inspiration, and motivation to assure program "take-off." Students of the community and observers of the profession know how difficult this is—even though journals, agency reports, and media publicity give evidence that it does occur from time to time.

Each era must find its own outlets for urgent social invention, and the present day is no exception. The task has become more difficult with increased standardization and formalization—despite some widespread experimentation with "community control" and other variations on "participatory administration." For, on the side of routinization there are legislation, administrative hierarchy, governmental guidelines and regulations, professionalization, "United Way" fund raising, and all other accouterments of a substantial public and voluntary social welfare development. The very expansion of social services tends to formalize the allocation of resources, the content of programs, delivery, and training. Real social invention comes from outside the system as "amateurs" develop new programs in response to experienced needs, from creative people within the system who break out of tradition periodically, and occasionally from the system itself, where it is organized to encourage diversity and change. With reference to the latter, administrative and organizational arrangements to promote diversity and some degree of decentralization or local option, and to admit into the system—at least experimentally—quite unorthodox programs are all essential. The social service history of the past decade indicates that circumstances such as these produced the movements and tendencies that are reflected in many programs today: "outreach" (bringing services and programs to clients who could not themselves seek or achieve access); "advocacy" (regarding as necessary those services which

champion entitlements and insist on access); consumer participation in policy development and service rendering; and service
localization.

Careful program evaluation, insofar as it focuses on the adequacy of specific service components (foster parent–child matching; counseling sessions with adolescents) or on total programs
(a particular agency dealing with drug abuse cases) may also
guide program reinforcement and reform. Experiments with market-
type devices (vouchers, supplying cash), which permit potential
consumers to "vote with their feet" and to select from among
options, will offer clues and encourage some innovations. Consumer cooperatives or community boards may invent services
meeting locally experienced need. We may anticipate important
innovations in the realm of public social utilities, a much underdeveloped field, as citizens from various backgrounds and economic classes find ways together to seek to enrich the quality of
life in their local communities. It is possible, too, to develop funding arrangements and policy participation so as to maximize the
proposals for social invention that might come from interest groups
as diverse as union members, "women's liberation," and students.

Innovation may be fostered by the acceptance of new social
service "hosts." Federal legislation in 1968 permitted unions to
bargain for day care as part of fringe-benefit packages, for example. Church groups, cooperative house owners, service clubs, and
industries may evolve public social utilities or case services out
of the needs of their unique constituencies and reflective of
unique cultural milieux. The result could be significant innovation,
a departure from the traditions in "freestanding" social services
and a new challenge to weave both adjunctive and "freestanding"
social services into a network. Or the alternative course may be
pursued by creating a separate network for the particular constituency: for workers in a union or industry, for residents of a
housing community, for members of a church.

A good rate of innovation cannot be expected unless there is a
reasonable degree of flexibility about theory as well. Any type of
conceptual orthodoxy, whether derived from Freudian psychiatry,
behavior-modification psychology, welfare economics, neo-Marxist
change strategies, or organizational sociology—to cite only a few
possibilities—blocks out some possibilities. Where the formal system may not be able to offer hospitality to innovation based on
unorthodox theory, the social service network must locate labora-

tories for research and development or experimentation, which are hospitable to change and invention. Ideally, many agencies should include among their staffs practitioner-scientists who, in interaction with direct practice, on the one hand, and the social policy thrusts of their time, on the other, can detect the need for and constantly seek new or revised service modalities.

Social services are today part of the standard of living. They are important "property" in a service society, urgent amenities in an urbanized civilization. Because program enacts policy and because social services sometimes implement policies whose consequences are unexplored, we have sought to introduce policy issues and to suggest their implications. Because programming determines the quality, availability, and effectiveness of service, we have highlighted approaches to systematic, efficient program development in the context of policy choice. Without exaggerating knowledge or skill, it is useful to note that increased rationality in social service planning and implementation may improve society's "buy" for money that is being spent and allow citizens to choose in the light of their priorities and preferences. These are reasonable preoccupations for a field whose very justification rests in the realms of the social minimum, social justice, and the creation of social solidarity.

NOTES

1. The listing that follows is derived from and elaborated in Alfred J. Kahn, et al., *Neighborhood Information Centers* (New York: Columbia University School of Social Work, 1966), pp. 112–119.
2. A survey of developments is presented in Alfred J. Kahn, Sheila B. Kamerman, and Brenda C. McGowan, *Child Advocacy: A National Baseline Study* (New York: Columbia University School of Social Work, 1972).
3. Elaine Cumming, *Systems of Social Regulations* (New York: Atherton, 1968).
4. See *Report of the Committee on Local Authority and Allied Social Services,* Cmnd. 3703 (London: Her Majesty's Stationery Office, 1968); or Alfred J. Kahn, *Studies in Social Policy and Planning* (New York: Russell Sage Foundation, 1969), pp. 278–290.
5. See Citizens' Committee for Children, *A Dream Deferred* (New York: The Committee, 1971), reprinted in *Child Welfare* for October 1971.
6. For elaboration, see Alfred J. Kahn, "Public Social Services: The Next Phase," *Public Welfare,* 30, 1 (Winter 1972), 15–24.

7. Edward J. O'Donnell and his collaborators, then in the Division of Intramural Research, Social and Rehabilitation Service, Department of Health, Education, and Welfare, have provided the most useful and comprehensive of the systematic reviews of general research in this field in a series of three articles in *Welfare in Review*: "Neighborhood Service Centers," October 1967; "The Neighborhood Service Center," January–February 1968; with Marilyn M. Sullivan, "Service Delivery and Social Action Through the Neighborhood Center," November–December 1969. An overview of a national survey of over 3,000 centers appears under the title, "The Multiservice Neighborhood Center: Preliminary Findings from a National Survey," by Edwin O'Donnell and Otto M. Reid, *Welfare in Review*, May–June, 1971, 1–8. See also "Service Integration: The Public Welfare Agency and The Multiservice Neighborhood Center," *Welfare in Review*, July–August 1971.

8. See the O'Donnell summaries and the related citations as well as Kahn, *Studies in Social Policy and Planning*, Chapter 7 and citations.

9. Robert Perlman and David Jones, *Neighborhood Service Centers* (Washington, D.C.: Government Printing Office, 1967).

10. O'Donnell cites the evidence.

11. For a report on a pioneering experience, see Harold Weisman (ed.), *Community Development in the Mobilization for Youth Experience* (New York: Association Press, 1969).

12. For a history of "reaching-out" projects in the 1950s, see Alfred J. Kahn, *Planning Community Services for Children in Trouble* (New York: Columbia University Press, 1963), Chapter 10.

13. For background and extensive bibliography, see Frances Fox Piven and Richard A. Cloward, *Regulating the Poor: The Functions of Public Welfare* (New York: Pantheon, 1971), Chapter 10.

14. On this, see Peter Marris and Martin Rein, *Dilemmas of Social Reform* (New York: Atherton, 1969); Martin Rein, "Poverty, Policy, and Purpose: The Dilemmas of Choice," *Social Policy: Issues of Choice and Change* (New York: Random House, 1970), pp. 221–248; Alfred J. Kahn, "The Anti-Poverty War as a Social Strategy," *Studies in Social Policy and Planning*, Chapter 2; and Sar Levitan, *The Great Society's Poor Law* (Baltimore: Johns Hopkins Press, 1969).

15. Charles E. Grosser, *Helping Youth—A Study of Six Community Organization Programs*, Office of Juvenile Delinquency and Youth Development, Department of Health, Education, and Welfare (Washington, D.C.: Government Printing Office, 1968), p. 57. For a full summary of experience, see O'Donnell and Sullivan, "Service Delivery and Social Action Through the Neighborhood Center"; and Perlman and Jones, *Neighborhood Service Centers*. Detailed documentation of limited service and the "pseudo-democratic" nature of many of the efforts at community control of antipoverty programs is offered in Ralph M. Kramer, *Participation of the Poor* (Englewood Cliffs, N.J.: Prentice-

Hall, 1969). Kramer identifies many positives in these programs even though they did not achieve the enunciated goals: control by the most disadvantaged poor and service improvement.

16. Norton Long, "The Local Community as an Ecology of Games," *American Journal of Sociology*, 64, 3 (November 1958), 251–261; also appears in several "urban readers" and anthologies. For a most helpful discussion of community control, growing out of experience on New York's Lower East Side, see Bertram M. Beck, "Community Control: A Distraction, Not an Answer," *Social Work*, 14, 4 (October 1969), 14–20; also, Neil Gilbert and Joseph W. Eaton, "Who Speaks for the Poor?" and Lisa Peattie, "Community Drama and Advocacy Planning," *Journal of the American Institute of Planners*, 36, 6 (November 1970), 411–416, 405–410.

17. For detail, see Marris and Rein, *Dilemmas of Social Reform*, and Alfred J. Kahn, "From Delinquency Treatment to Community Development," in Paul F. Lazarsfeld, William H. Sewell, and Harold L. Wilensky, *The Uses of Sociology* (New York: Basic Books, 1967), pp. 477–505.

18. On this, see S. M. Miller and Warner Bloomberg, Jr., "Epilogue: Shall the Poor Always Be Impoverished," in Warner Bloomberg, Jr., and Henry J. Schmandt (eds.), *Power, Poverty and Urban Policy*, Vol. II of *Urban Affairs Annual Review* (Berkeley, Calif.: Sage Publications, 1968), pp. 565–577; also Alfred J. Kahn, "Do Social Services Have a Future in New York?" constituting the *City Almanac* (New York: New School for Social Research, February 1971).

Reading List

The following will be of special interest to both concerned citizens and students. Each contains further bibliography, as do the footnotes in the present volume.

Bloedorn, Jack C., et al. *Designing Social Service Systems.* Chicago: American Public Welfare Association, 1970.

Carter, Genevieve W. "The Challenge of Accountability—How We Measure the Outcome of Our Efforts," *Public Welfare,* 29, 3 (Summer 1971), 267–277.

Cumming, Elaine. *Systems of Social Regulation.* New York: Atherton, 1968.

Encyclopedia of Social Work, Sixteenth Issue. New York: National Association of Social Workers, 1971.

Handler, Joel, and **Ellen Jane Hollingsworth.** *The "Deserving Poor": A Study of Welfare Administration.* Chicago: Markham Publishing Co., 1971.

Jeffreys, Margot. *An Anatomy of Social Welfare Services.* London: Michael Joseph, 1965

Kahn, Alfred J. *Theory and Practice of Social Planning.* New York: Russell Sage Foundation, 1969.

————. *Studies in Social Policy and Planning.* New York: Russell Sage Foundation, 1969.

Kershaw, Joseph. *Government Against Poverty.* Chicago: Markham Publishing Co., 1970.

Lally, Dorothy. *National Social Service Systems.* Washington, D.C.: Department of Health, Education, and Welfare, 1970.

Levitan, Sar. *The Great Society's Poor Law.* Baltimore: Johns Hopkins Press, 1969.

Maas, Henry S. (ed.). *Research in the Social Services: A Five Year Review.* New York: National Association of Social Workers, 1971.

Merriam, Ida C., and **Alfred M. Skolnick.** *Social Welfare Expenditures Under Public Programs in the United States, 1929–66.* Research Report no. 25, Office of Research and Statistics, Social Security Administration. Washington, D.C.: Government Printing Office, 1968.

Perlman, Robert, and **David Jones.** *Neighborhood Service Centers.* Washington, D.C.: Government Printing Office, 1967.

Rein, Martin. *Social Policy.* New York: Random House, 1970.

Report of the Committee on Local Authority and Allied Social Services. Cmnd. 3703. London: Her Majesty's Stationery Office, 1968.

Rivlin, Alice. *Systematic Thinking for Social Action.* Washington, D.C.: The Brookings Institution, 1971.

Robson, William A., and **Bernard Crick** (eds.). *The Future of the Social Services.* Baltimore: Penguin, 1970.

Schon, Donald A. "The Blindness System," *The Public Interest,* No. 18 (Winter 1970), 25–38.

Schorr, Alvin. *Explorations in Social Policy.* New York: Basic Books, 1968.

Scott, Robert A. *The Making of Blind Men.* New York: Russell Sage Foundation, 1968.

Steiner, Gilbert Y. *The State of Welfare.* Washington, D.C.: The Brookings Institution, 1971.

Titmuss, Richard M. *Commitment to Welfare.* New York: Pantheon, 1968.
————————. *The Gift Relationship.* New York: Pantheon, 1971.

Townsend, Peter, et al. *The Fifth Social Service.* London: Fabian Society, 1970.

Willmott, Phyllis. *Consumer's Guide to the British Social Services.* Baltimore: Penguin, 1971.

Younghusband, Eileen, et al. *Living with Handicap.* London: The National Bureau for Co-operation in Child Care, 1970.

Index

paradigm, general, lacking, 129–30

public health conceptualizations, 139–41, 142

systems approaches, 142–6

multiservice centers, *see* Storefronts and multiservice centers

mutual aid, 13, 21, 32–3, 184–5

Myrdal, G., 98

Nader, R., 73

National Center for Voluntary Action, 53

needs

resource allocation and, 60–2

test, universalism and, 81–2

neighborhood information centers, 31, 164–6

advocacy services, 168, 169

elements in program of, 166–8

social action and, 183–4

networks, social service

access services, 150–1, 161–71

boundaries, definition of, 150

case integration, 152–3

coordination, 152–3, 172

eligibility assessment, 151–2

freestanding vs. formalization concepts, 154–5

intervention repertoire, 152

model, 149–50

reporting and evaluation in, 153

specialization vs. integration, 155–7

storefronts and multiservice centers, 174–80

see also Specific services

"new property" concept, 84, 87–8

Nixon, R. M., 4, 26, 100

non-market criteria, 21–2, 25

nonpublic agencies, 101–6

see also Voluntary agencies

O'Donnell, E., 175, 178*n*, 180, 186

Office of Economic Opportunity (OEO), 41, 81, 119*n*

operations research, 125–9

programming model and, 143

opportunity programs, 98, 99

outreach, 167, 191

participation, community, 32–3, 51

community identification and representation, 187–8

control of services and, 185–9

professional and consumer roles, issue of, 186–7

social action, direct services and, 182–5

systems approach and, 147

performance contracting, 105–6, 118–20, 148

personnel, 44, 46, 51–3

formalization vs. participatory administration, 120–5

storefronts and multiservice centers, 175, 176–7, 178–9

voluntary agencies, 52–3

policy, social, 26–7, 28–9, 69–88

administration, participatory vs. formalized, 120–5

case services concept, 76–7

cash, vouchers, or benefits-in-kind, 111–18

concern with, development of, 70–4

consumption vs. investment concepts, 95–100

cost-benefit research, 125–32

costs and, 80–3

efficiency rating and, 125–9

evaluation of services and, 54–60

exceptionalism, 83–4

institutional view, 77–8

DATE

DEMCO 38-297